Quiet Amsterdam

Siobhan Wall

FRANCES LINCOLN LIMITED
PUBLISHERS

Quiet Amsterdam

Siobhan Wall

Frances Lincoln Limited
4 Torriano Mews
Torriano Avenue
London NW5 2RZ
www.franceslincoln.com

Quiet Amsterdam
Copyright © Frances Lincoln Limited 2012
Text and photographs copyright © Siobhan Wall 2012
Map by Maria Charalambous

First Frances Lincoln edition 2012

A catalogue record for this book is available from the British Library.

978-0-7112-3342-3

Printed and bound in China

1 2 3 4 5 6 7 8 9

Cover Brouwersgracht; back cover Museum van Loon;
p.1 Sunhead of 1617; p.2–3 In de Waag; this page Zuid Zeeland;
p.9 Tassenmuseum garden

Contents

Introduction

It may seem surprising to publish a book about quiet, tranquil places in one of the liveliest cities in western Europe, but there are many reasons why *Quiet Amsterdam* came into being. When I moved to the Netherlands a few years ago, I decided to explore the city by taking photographs of undiscovered places. I would write in the mornings then go out in the afternoon with just a map, my camera and my notebook. Like the Situationists in 1960s Paris, I wanted to *derivé*, to wander without a definite plan and see where I ended up. I often found myself in unusual places well off the beaten track – like the lush, overgrown nature garden in Westerpark where I was hidden by tall, waving reeds. Most days, I got on the best form of transport for the Dutch landscape – my 25-year-old trustworthy bicycle – and just set off . . .

I cycled to little-known lakes and unfamiliar parks, even when it was snowing, because Amsterdam looks really beautiful in winter. What was most pleasurable was finding things I hadn't expected. Maps can't tell you about the amazing field of shaggy headed flowers in Erasmuspark, for example, or the strange 'skritch, skritch' noise made by the ice skaters' blades on a frozen pond. My travels were often interrupted by serendipitous moments – seeing two swans flying about the Diem Lake near Ijburg and a semi-camouflaged hare crouching in the undergrowth alongside De Poel Lake. I also remember the croaking frogs in the dyke in Holysloot, which were so noisy they made me laugh. (This pretty village is the only location that took more than an hour to cycle to. Everywhere else in this book is accessible from Central Station within 45 minutes by tram, bus or bicycle).

So, why produce the second edition of a book about where to find quiet places in Amsterdam? Although

Amsterdam is a beautiful place with great cafes and restaurants, and is a fascinating city where hundreds of lively cultural events take place each year, I've discovered that many people still find the city noisy and crowded. From squealing brakes at Central Station to loud disco music at the occasional Dam Square funfair, the city still has its own unwelcome cacophonies. In a lively capital city with hundreds of shops, nearly forty museums, a thousand restaurants and over four million visitors a year, peace and quiet are still difficult to find. The first edition of *Quiet Amsterdam* was popular, which was very encouraging, as I realised I wasn't the only person who appreciated tranquil places. Journalists and even one or two broadcasters are starting to alert their readers and viewers to the problems of excessive and unwanted noise in the places we live, work and spend our free time. More and more researchers are addressing this problem and scientific reports have shown that excessive or constant noise can be exhausting and eventually lead to stress-related disorders. It's also obvious that loud music in bars and cafes makes it very hard for people to talk to one another. 'Pipedown' (the British campaign against piped music) describes unwanted 'muzac' as one of the 'under-recognised scourges of contemporary life', which suggests that despite all our attempts to screen out unwanted noise, it is still difficult to find oases of calm in big cities. Even governments are increasingly aware of the need for quietness in everyday life. The UK Department for the Environment and Rural Affairs (DEFRA) developed a 'Noise Policy' which has led to some valuable studies on the impact of noise levels on people in both urban and rural areas and European cities with a population of over 250,000 are now required to compile maps of quiet areas and make these accessible to the public.

Aware of how noisy the city could be, I began taking photographs of tranquil and inspiring parks, gardens, little shops and any other places to escape from daily stress and noise. On my travels I discovered that many locations have a fascinating history. I learnt about how the initials of the former owners were an integral part of the design in the Museum van Loon's magnificent brass staircase, for example. I came across picturesque landscapes as well as some strange places, including Diemer Vijfhoek, with its deserted ponds and isolated rocky shoreline. Entranced by overgrown graveyards, deserted woods and still ponds, I realised that photographs might entice readers away away from the crowded city centre towards some less familiar but amazing hidden parks and wild spaces.

Unlike typical sightseeing guides, *Quiet Amsterdam* invites a gentle gaze and patient looking, closer to the unhurried consumption of culinary delights proposed by the slow food movement than the fast thrills of the red light district. I was often reminded that it is not only people with hearing problems who would benefit from finding quiet(er) restaurants to meet friends. Knowing that I was working on *Quiet Amsterdam*, I was often asked to recommend less busy places to eat and drink, so I was pleased to find a few cafes and restaurants which still don't play recorded music.

There were other ways in which I realised that I wasn't alone in appreciating quiet places. I often saw people sitting on benches reading, others walking their dogs along riverside paths and, even in the middle of winter, a lone cyclist on the tree-lined avenue alongside the Noordhollandsch Kanaal. It is also worth remembering that at certain times of the day even busy places can be quiet, as on Sunday morning, when almost everyone in Amsterdam is still asleep. This is the perfect time to wander past 17th-century houses along the canals or visit a small museum.

Whilst taking photographs for the book, I also realised that I'd begun to develop a hidden agenda, inspired by belonging to an intrepid cycling group when I first moved to Amsterdam: perhaps such adventurousness represented an idea of freedom that is rarely 'advertised'. For instance, Amsterdam Noord, which is reached by ferry across Het IJ, is rarely visited by tourists but has some unexpectedly beautiful parks. These unpretentious green spaces are not really places to 'see or be seen', but places to walk or cycle through, almost invisibly. So, instead of insisting that you spend money in department stores or lively bars, this book gives implicit permission for anyone to wander off on their own, to discover their own quiet, hidden paths and the potential solace of undisturbed places. I became increasingly aware of the relevance of John Urry's comments in *The Tourist Gaze* (1990). He describes the prevalence of shopping centres with their attendant security guards and 'delimited space': 'Developments of this sort also represent the changing nature of public space in contemporary societies. An increasingly central role is being played by privately owned and controlled consumption spaces.' Instead of feeling deterred by the presence of high levels of surveillance, the places in *Quiet Amsterdam* are often beyond the intrusive gaze of the closed circuit TV camera. If 'certain types of behaviour . . . such as not sitting on the floor' are expected in shopping malls and pedestrianised city centres, the open parks and semi-wild spaces in this book invite instead 'oppositional cultural practice[s]'. For me, this includes wandering without purpose, going out without a shopping list and lingering somewhere without any intention except to sit on the grass and just listen.

In fact, many shopping streets in large cities now don't have many places to sit down. Dam Square has only around twelve seats and Kalverstraat, the Oxford Street of Amsterdam, has no seats at all. Shoppers who want to rest their feet are meant to queue up in crowded cafes; there is nowhere to lie on the grass and gaze at the sky. So, this book has an implicit social agenda; it subtly clamours for more opportunites for people of all ages to sit and talk, read or ponder in cities.

As a former university lecturer, I really enjoy finding new books but the new OBA public library in Amsterdam is now so busy that it wasn't included in this second edition. Many of us will be delighted that a library is now the star attraction in a city, but this means it's just a bit too popular for a guide to quiet places. There are some incredibly well-stocked libraries in Amsterdam – most of which, like the Royal Tropical Institute Library next to Oosterpark, seem underused. I hope this book will encourage more readers to seek them out.

This second edition also includes information about accessibility – a problem in old Dutch houses with their steep wooden stairs. There are a few places which can accommodate wheelchair users and it might be useful to know that booster scooters (three- or four-wheeled electric mobility vehicles) can be rented for a week from Vegro, at Bilderdijkstraat 132, a shop that caters for people who have mobility problems. A driving licence is not needed to rent these, but a passport and deposit are required at the time of booking – ask for a scootmobiel. Visit www.vegro.info or call their freephone number +31 (0)800 288 7766. The 'Accessible Amsterdam' website also gives useful information about transport for people who use a wheelchair or have a disability: www.toegankelijkamsterdam.nl.

Readers of Dutch might be interested to know of Stichting Bam, an organisation which campaigns against music in public spaces, including shops and cafes: www.stopdemuziekte.nu ('Stop the Music Now').

The following websites might also be inspiring: www.ukna.org.uk; www.slowfood.com; www.pipedown.info.

The map that follows serves as a guide to the location of each entry, numbered in the order they appear in the book.

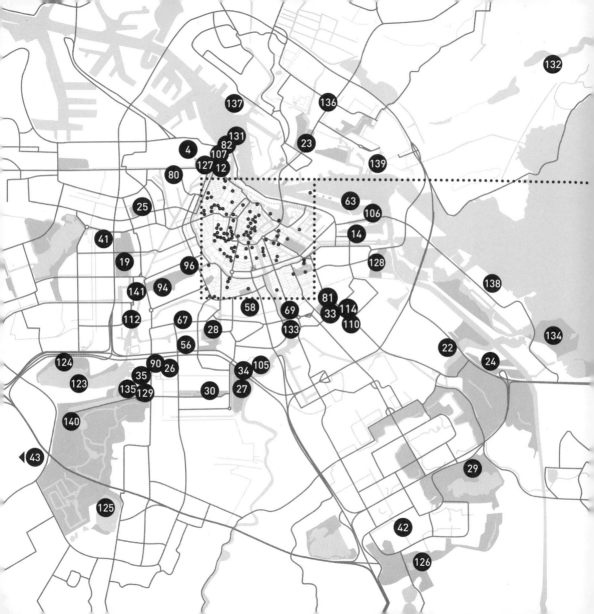

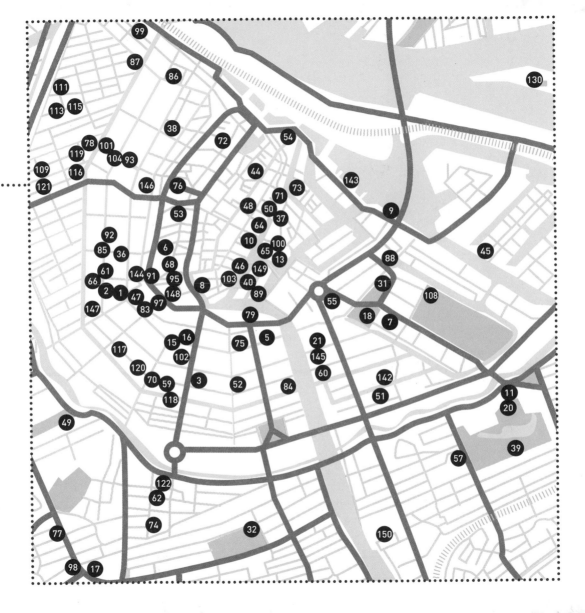

Museums

① Bijbelsmuseum

Herengracht 366–368 ☎ (020) 624 2436
€ www.bijbelsmuseum.nl
Open Monday–Saturday 10am–5pm, Sunday and most public
holidays 11am–5pm, closed 1 January, 30 April but open
Christmas Day and Boxing Day
Tram 1, 2, 5 to Spui
The building is partially wheelchair accessible

Not only is it worth visiting this pair of converted gentleman's
canal houses for the handsome staircase and marble hallway,
there is also a beautiful garden full of almond trees and a
modern rectangular pond where you can hear the gentle sound
of trickling water. The listed buildings were built in 1662 by
the famous architect Philips Vingboons, in a style known as
Dutch Classicism. There is also a fascinating historic kitchen
and an exquisite ceiling painted in 1718 by Jacob de Wit in the
room overlooking the garden. The temporary exhibitions are
consistently engaging and the history of bibles from different
lands really interesting. In one corner of the building there are
two 'aroma cabinets' where you can lift the stoppers on small
phials to smell various herbs and spices such as incense and
myrrh. After wandering round the garden, you can enjoy a quiet
coffee in a sun-filled room at the rear of the building.

② Huis Marseille

Foundation for Photography, Keizersgracht 401 ☎ (020) 531 8989
€ www.huismarseille.nl
Open Tuesday–Sunday 11am–6pm, closed on 1 January, 30 April, 25 December and when exhibitions are being hung
Tram 1, 2, 5 to Keizersgracht
The building is wheelchair accessible

This very impressive former gentleman's residence is now one of the best locations in Amsterdam for contemporary and archival photography. Each room is a beautifully proportioned space in which to view sophisticated and intelligent artworks. Exhibitions have included Dutch photographers such as Marnix Goosens and Jacqueline Hassink as well as South African documentarist David Goldblatt. There is also a small media room for use by visitors with current photography journals and a coffee machine. Upstairs, you can read catalogues and other photobooks in a very pleasant library with views over the formal garden.

3 Museum van Loon

Keizersgracht 672 ☎ (020) 624 5255
€ www.museumvanloon.nl
Open Wednesday–Monday 11am–5pm, closed 1 January, 30 April, 25 December
Tram 4, 16, 24, 25 to Keizersgracht
The building is not accessible for wheelchair users

Museum van Loon was built in 1672 and the first resident was Ferdinand Bol, one of Rembrandt van Rijn's better-known pupils. In the 19th century the van Loon family moved in and remodelled the brass staircase, ensuring that their initials were included in the curlicue designs. This very grand but welcoming museum hosts a magnificent collection of van Loon family portraits, silverware and porcelain from the 18th century. In addition to the sumptuous bedcoverings and exuberant wallpaper, look out for the unusual wooden candelabra in the dining room. The museum also has a beautiful garden which was renovated thirty years ago using designs from a 17th-century map of Amsterdam. This is a delightful place to sit in the warmer months of the year but it is also charming during the colder seasons.

④ Museum Het Schip

Spaarndammerplantsoen 140
☎ (020) 418 2885
€ www.hetschip.nl
Open Tuesday–Sunday 11am–5pm
Bus 22 to Spaarndammerbuurt
Wheelchair access is possible in
the museum but not upstairs in the
former workers' apartment

Not all the museums in Amsterdam
show how the wealthy and privileged
lived. This building used to be a
post office and the large complex
was built as model housing for
city workers. Designed by Michel
de Klerk in the early 20th century
in the Amsterdam School style of
architecture, the three apartment
blocks in the Spaarndammer area
are still inhabited by local residents.
The rooms have been well preserved
so that details such as the grey-blue
tiled public telephone booths are still
intact. Round the corner is a carefully
restored working class apartment
and visitors can not only get to see a
typical 1920s Dutch interior complete
with old children's toys and kitchen
implements, but also the remarkable
wooden structure inside the
distinctive brick tower.

The nearby Het Schip lunchroom
is open to 5.30pm.

⑤ Museum Willet-Holthuysen

Herengracht 605 ☎ (020) 523 1822
€ www.willetholthuysen.nl
Open Monday–Friday 10am–5pm,
Saturday, Sunday and public holidays
11am–5pm, closed 1 January, 30 April,
25 December
Tram 9, 14 to Rembrantplein
The museum is wheelchair accessible

Amsterdam boasts a number of canal
house museums and this is one of
the most spectacular. The basement
entrance leads on to the former kitchen
and is full of glass cabinets of Delftware
and other objets d'art. Upstairs, there
are some impressive period rooms
where visitors can find inlaid armoires,
marble portrait busts and stunning
flower still lifes. The intriguing small
leaded windows at the rear of the
museum look over a formal garden
with gravel pathways and box hedges.
This museum is an ideal place to spend
a leisurely afternoon amongst precious
objects from former eras.

6 Amsterdam Museum

Kalverstraat 92 ☎ (020) 523 1822
€ www.amsterdammuseum.nl
Open Monday–Friday 10am–5pm, weekends and public holidays 11am–5pm, closed 1 January, 30 April, 25 December
Tram 1, 2, 4, 5, 9, 16, 24, 25 to either Spui stop
The museum is wheelchair accessible

Housed in a former orphanage, this impressive collection of 18th-century buildings is now a large museum showing the history of Amsterdam. The museum also has engaging temporary exhibitions on subjects relating to Amsterdam life and most information panels have English text. The shop is a useful place to buy gifts for friends back home and has some informative guides to the city. The nearby David and Goliath cafe doesn't play music but can get crowded at weekends so tends to be a bit noisy.

⑦ Hollandsche Schouwburg

Plantage Middenlaan 24 ☎ (020) 531 0830
Free www.hollandscheschouwburg.nl
Open every day from 11am–4pm except for Yom Kippur and the Jewish New Year
Tram 9, 14 to Plantage Kerklaan
The building is wheelchair accessible

This former 19th-century theatre was used by the occupying Nazis during the Second World War as an assembly point before deporting Jewish people to Camp Westerbork and concentration camps elsewhere in Europe. The main auditorium is now a monument to the 104,000 people who were killed, whilst on the first floor there is a permanent exhibition about how the discriminatory laws affected the Jewish community as well as documentation about the deportations. Information about how a few Jewish children were saved can be seen in the exhibition space upstairs. In addition, visitors can read nearly 7,000 surnames of Jewish families who were deported from the Netherlands, inscribed in the memorial hall to the left of the entrance.

8 Special Collections Library, University of Amsterdam

Oude Turfmarkt 129 ☎ (020) 525 7300
Free www.bc.uba.uva.nl **Open** Exhibition rooms Tuesday–Friday 10am–5pm, Saturday and Sunday 1pm–5pm, closed on bank holidays and 30 April, New Year's Day, Easter Sunday, Ascension Day, Whit Sunday and Christmas Day
Tram 4, 9, 14, 16, 24, 25
The building is wheelchair accessible and has adapted toilets

The impressive exhibition space within the University of Amsterdam Special Collections Library was designed by the architects Atelier Pro and Merkx+Girod a few years ago and is a welcome addition to the city. The library organises about three temporary exhibitions each year, enabling visitors to see some of the extraordinary publications and artefacts rarely displayed in public. Previous exhibitions included 'Ape, Fish, Book', the presentation of texts by and about the 18th-century Swedish taxonomist Linneaus as well as illustrated works by his successors. This is an excellent place to see some of the world's most fascinating maps, drawings, photographs and written texts; from medieval manuscripts to innovative book designs.

9 Arcam

Prins Hendrikkade 600 ☎ (020) 620 4878
Free www.arcam.nl
Open Tuesday–Saturday 1pm–5pm
Bus 22, 42, 43 to Kadijksplein or a 15-minute walk from Central Station
There is wheelchair access throughout the building

From the city side, this unusual building looks as if a large piece of grey corrugated iron has been bent into a curved tent and then pushed into the ground. Inside, it is a surprisingly light and welcoming exhibition space where visitors can see temporary exhibitions about the work of Dutch architects and other urban planning projects. Unlike most museums and public exhibition spaces in Amsterdam, entrance is free.

Libraries

⑩ Bushuis Library

Kloveniersburgwal 48 ☎ (020) 525 2403
€ annual membership fee to borrow books but free to visit
www.uba.uva.nl
Open Monday–Thursday 9am–7.30pm, Friday 9am–5pm, with
reduced hours outside term time
Metro Nieuwmarkt – take the Nieuwe Hoogstraat exit and turn left,
turn left again into Kloveniersburgwal and the library is on the right
The building is wheelchair accessible

Originally built in 1603 as the East India House for the VOC and
then used as an arms depot, this grand building was rebuilt at the
end of the 19th century in the Gothic style. The impressive 'pepper
door' dates from the Golden Age, but inside, the library is efficient
and modern. The building opened as a university library in 2001 and
houses mainly books for political, social and cultural sciences. A
good place to work is in the computer room in the huge attic, which
offers the rare combination of dark wooden medieval beams and
the latest internet technology.

🔟 KIT Library

Mauritskade 63 ☎ (020) 568 8246 / 8462
€ annual membership fee to borrow books but free to visit
www.kit.nl **Open** Monday–Thursday 10am–5pm **Tram** 9, 10,
14 to Alexanderplein **Bus** 22 to Eerste van Swindenstraat
The library is wheelchair accessible

This impressive library is part of KIT, the Royal Tropical
Institute; an 'independent centre of knowledge in the
areas of international and intercultural cooperation.' Walk
through the unusual marbled hallway to reach the first
floor reading room which houses 250,000 publications
and journals on health, gender, education, economics
and other subjects concerning developing countries.

🔢 Fonds BKVB Reading Room

Brouwersgracht 276 ☎ (020) 523 1523 **Free**
www.fondsbkvb.nl **Open** Monday–Friday 10am–5pm
Tram 3 or **Bus** 21, 22 to Harlemmerplein
The library and exhibition space are wheelchair accessible

This high ceilinged space is one of the quietest places to
read in the city. Located on one of the loveliest canals in
Amsterdam, the Fonds BKVB bookshelves are brightly
coloured and heaving with books on contemporary art and
architecture, but everything is reference only. There's also
a shelf of current art journals, and two exhibition spaces
on the ground floor where work by up-and-coming artists
can be seen throughout the year.

⑬ Pintohuis

Sint Antoniebreestraat 69 ☎ (020) 624 3184
€ annual membership fee to borrow books but free to visit
www.oba.nl
Open Monday 2pm–8pm, Wednesday 10am–5.30pm, Friday 10am–5.30pm, Saturday 11am–4pm
Metro Nieuwmarkt
No disabled access to the upper floor (poetry books and temporary exhibitions)

This small library was the former home of a wealthy Jewish Portuguese banker, Isaac de Pinto. Built in 1671, it is atmospheric and has a nice, carved wood staircase and a small exhibition room upstairs for local artists to show their work. There are many novels in English on the ground floor, and a good children's section to the rear.

14 IISH Library

Cruquiusweg 31 ☎ (020) 668 5866
€ annual membership fee to borrow books but free to visit
www.iisg.nl **Open** Monday–Friday 9am–5pm (last requests for books 4pm)
Tram 7 to Molukkenstraat, 14 to Javaplein **Bus** 43, 65 to Cruquiusweg
The library and the Press Museum next door both have access for wheelchair users

Don't be deterred by its rather grey, ominous looking exterior. The library of the International Institute for Social History overlooks a modern harbour so offers a panoramic view of contemporary Dutch architecture. There are a few surprises in the huge IISH collection, including an early edition of Thomas More's *Utopia* and the private letters of the suffragette Sylvia Pankhurst. The library also contains a huge collection of communist propaganda posters so this is a good resource for graphic designers or anyone interested in the relationship between labour history and 20th-century visual art.

⓯ Goethe Institute Library

Herengracht 470 ☎ (020) 531 2900
€ annual membership fee to borrow books but free to visit
www.goethe.de/ins/nl/ams/
Open Tuesday–Thursday 12.30pm–6.30pm
Tram 16, 24, 25 to Keizersgracht
The garden and library are wheelchair accessible but not the classrooms on the second floor

Primarily intended for students learning German, there is limited public access to the magnificent garden behind this canalside building. Not only does the Goethe Institut run a cultural programme focusing on German culture, there is also a library in this handsome Herengracht mansion. Even if you don't read the language, there are interesting CDs and videos for loan.

⑯ Aletta

Vijzelstraat 20 ☎ (020) 665 0820
€ annual membership fee to borrow books but free to visit
www.aletta.nu **Open** Tuesday–Friday 10am–5pm
Tram 4, 9, 14, 24, 26 to Muntplein
The building is wheelchair accessible

Aletta recently relocated to central Amsterdam and this international women's archive is an ideal place to spend time doing research. For a small annual fee, publications can be loaned out and even posted to locations outside Amsterdam. In addition to their many books on women's history and literature, the archive also includes scrapbooks and personal letters, including photographs of Aletta Jacobs, the library's namesake. Jacobs (1854–1929) was not only the first Dutch woman to study at university she was also the first to qualify and work as a doctor. She is renowned for supporting women at a time when their options were very limited.

⑰ Roelof Hartplein Library

Roelof Hartplein 430 ☎ (020) 662 0094
€ annual membership fee to borrow books but free to visit
www.oba.nl **Open** Monday 2pm–8pm, Wednesday, Friday 10am–5.30pm, Thursday 10am–8pm, Saturday 11am–4pm
Tram 3, 12, 24 to Roelof Hartplein
The library has wheelchair access

This public library, clearly visible at the junction of J.M. Coenenstraat, has the feel of a gentlemen's club, with wide, old wooden tables and large chairs, making it a good place to read the paper and browse the shelves. Afterwards, find time for scones and jam at Bakkerswinkel, just round the corner; one of the best tea rooms in Amsterdam.

Parks, gardens and nature reserves

18 Hortus Botanicus

Plantage Middenlaan 2 ☎ tel (020) 625 9021
€ www.hortus.nl
Open Monday–Friday 9am–5pm, Saturday, Sunday and bank holidays
10am–5pm, stays open late in July and August, closes at 4pm in winter,
and closed 1 January, 25 December
Tram 9, 14 to Mr Visserplein **Metro** Waterlooplein, take the Hortus exit,
turn right and walk along the canal
The garden is wheelchair accessible except for the elevated walkways in
the glasshouses

This compact and densely planted green space in the centre of Amsterdam
is one of the oldest botanic gardens in the world. Since 1682 plants have
been grown here for medicinal or educational purposes, and around fifteen
years ago an all-weather three-climate greenhouse was constructed. There
are over four thousand species, including the very rare, prehistoric Wollemi
Pine, recently discovered in Australia. The former orangery is now a mobile
phone-free restaurant serving mainly organic food and has a lovely terrace to
sit outside in warm weather. The garden can become crowded during summer
evenings when locals gather to watch the extraordinary Victoria plant bloom
in the round pond. Otherwise, the palm house, sunken pond and winding paths
still remain peaceful.

19 Rembrandtpark

Entrances on Einsteinweg, Orteliuskade and Postjeskade
Free www.nieuwwest.amsterdam.nl **Open** all hours
Tram 13 to Jan Evertsenstraat or 1, 17 to Cornelis Lelylaan
There is disabled access throughout the park

This city park runs along the Postjeswetering canal and
has some pleasant cycle routes running through it. There
are some eye-catching modern bridges over streams
and even a loud pop (free) outdoor gym. Instead of loud pop
music, you can keep fit whilst listening to birdsong in the
open air. There's even a small hilly area near the Cornelis
Lelylaan entrance for al-fresco lunches or a gentle stroll
at dusk.

20 Oosterpark

Entrances at Linneausstraat, Oosterparkstaat and
Beukersweg ☎ (0) 627 431705 Mr Sifu Chan € for tai-chi
classes www.taopai.nl **Open** classes every day from
10am–11am, except 25 December
Tram 9 or **Bus** 22 to Eerste van Swindenstraat
The park is wheelchair accessible

This lovely park dating from the 1890s was designed
in the 'English style' and has wooded paths along the
perimeter and a tranquil pond. It is particularly nice in
June when the heady scent of lime blossom fills the air.
Every morning, a gentle outdoor tai-chi class is held by
the bandstand and anyone can join in.

21 Amstelhoven

Between Nieuwe Keizersgracht 1A and Nieuwe Herengracht 18 **Free**
Open daily 9am–5pm (it seems to open later than specified at the weekend, however)
Metro Waterlooplein **Tram** 9, 14 to Waterlooplein, walk south along the left side of the Amstel then turn right down the south side of Nieuwe Herengracht
The garden paths are suitable for wheelchairs

Not many people know about this secret garden next to the Hermitage Museum, the 18th-century almshouse, which, until it was converted into a museum a few years ago, had been in continuous use for over two hundred years as a nursing home. Walking round, you'll see a rectangular pond with a floating globe and a few unremarkable outdoor sculptures. On the canal side is the Outsider Art Shop where artists with learning disabilities sell their artwork.

(22) Pen Bos, Diemen

Entrance at Diemerpolderweg **Free**
Open all day, every day
Tram 9 to Diemen Sniep and walk around 20 minutes south **Bus** 66 to Diemerparklaan
The paths are wheelchair accessible

Hardly anyone knows about Pen Bos, the area of open woodland to the east of Amsterdam. This is possibly because it's at the end of tramline 9 so there are only a few people wandering along the footpaths in this pretty nature reserve. Named after the tiny River Diem, which used to run though this typically flat Dutch landscape, this area is a delightful place to take a walk in the midst of winter when the trees are covered in frost. It is very easy to find – cycle east out of the city along Middenweg and carry on until you get to Muiderstraatweg. On the left is Overdiemenweg, a small road just after the Diemer Ijsclub building. Small footpaths branch off to the right surrounded by tall reeds and ash trees.

㉓ Noorderpark

Entrances on Wingerdweg, Buiksloterdijk and the
Oeverlanderoute cycle path ☎ (020) 634 9934 **Free**
www.noorderpark.amsterdam.nl **Open** all hours
Ferry Buiksloterweg free ferry 51 to Amsterdam Noord,
then cycle along the Buiksloterweg path to Noorderpark
The paths are wheelchair accessible

Tall trees line the cycle path along the Noordhollandsch
Kanaal which runs through the northern suburb above Het
IJ. There are some lovely windswept views of the water
and in winter, with just a few seagulls flying overhead, it
can feel as if you are the only person around. Formerly the
Florapark, this green area was recently renovated.

㉔ Diemerbos

Main entrance on Weteringweg, just off Stammerdijk **Free**
Open all hours **Tram** 9 to the end of the line, then walk
towards Penbos along Muiderstraatweg
Wide paths provide disabled access

Diemerbos is a huge area (around 200 hectares) of
grassland and small trees in-between Weesp, Diemen
and Amsterdam Zuid-Oost. It's a relatively young nature
reserve as most trees were planted around ten years ago,
so it feels very open and safe. There are clearly marked
paths, bridleways and cycle routes amongst the low lying
woodland and it is much less densely populated by visitors
than the Amsterdamse Bos.

25 Erasmuspark

Entrance on Jan van Galenstraat, corner of Vespuccistraat
Free Open 7am–9pm April and October, 7am–10pm May
and September, 7am–11pm June and August, until dusk
at other times **Tram** 7, 12, 14 to Jan van Galenstraat, 13 to
Marco Polostraat
The park has disabled access throughout

Named after 15th-century humanist Desiderius Erasmus,
this park has an astounding flower garden, as well as
benches and tables with inlaid chequerboard designs to play
chess and other games in the open air. It is especially nice to
walk round the tree-lined perimeter, as being surrounded by
water on four sides, it is almost a green inner-city island.

26 VU Botanic Garden

Entrance at Van der Boechorststraat 8
www.vuamsterdam.com **Free**
Open Monday–Friday 8am–4.30pm (due to close in 2015)
Metro 51 to Arent Janszoon Ernststraat
The garden is wheelchair accessible

Unlike the better-known botanic garden in the centre of
town, entrance to the more modern VU (Vrije Universiteit)
green space is free. Established in 1967, it was intended for
use as a research and education centre for biology students
at the university. The garden is renowned for its bonsai
collection and there are a few turtles in a pond inside one
of the glasshouses so worth a visit even in winter.

㉗ Amstelpark

Europaboulevard ☎ (020) 644 4216
www.amstelparkart.nl **Free**
Open 8am to half an hour before sunset
Metro or **Tram** 4 to RAI then a 5-minute walk **Bus** 62 to Europaboulevard
The Amstel park has wide paths suitable for wheelchairs and mobility vehicles

This large, spacious park on the edge of the city is particularly quiet in winter as no bicycles are allowed inside the gates. Away from the miniature golf and children's train ride, the pine tree glade is a lovely place to sit in warmer weather. There is also a modern gallery called Het Glazen Huis (the Glasshouse), which shows temporary art exhibitions. Nearby is a magnificent rhododendron garden, which provides some stunning natural colour in the summer.

28 Beatrixpark

Entrances on Diepenbrockstraat, De Groene Zoom path from RAI station, or Beethovenstraat
www.vriendenbeatrixpark.nl **Free**
Open all day, every day **Tram** 12, 25 to Scheldestraat (a 5-minute walk) or 4 to RAI (a 7-minute walk)
The park is fully accessible (but don't rely on the toilet being open except on summer afternoons)

Beatrixpark is an idyllic green space on the edge of the city. There are wooded glades and gently sloping grassy banks overlooking the water – just perfect for quiet picnics. It was originally landscaped to ensure that only a partial view could be seen from any vantage point, so any surrounding buildings are hidden by huge chestnut and oak trees. Apparently a couple of rare sparrowhawks were hatching in the Nordic pines, but you are more likely to see bright green screeching parakeets or still, grey herons near the round pond. One of the loveliest corners of the park is the Artsenijhof, the medicinal plant garden on the eastern edge near Wielengenstraat.

Local shops for picnic food include Natuurwinkel on Scheldestraat which has organic fruit juices, sunflower seed bread and specialist Dutch cheeses.

29 Gaasperpark

Main entrance on Loosdrechtdreef
☎ (020) 641 0404 **Free**
Open all hours **Metro** 53 to Gaasperplas
The paths are wheelchair accessible

Originally designed for the Floriade garden exhibition in 1982, this large park consists of grassland and sandy beaches surrounding the Gaasperplas Lake. To the north it's more wooded and you are less likely to find families picnicking by the water. Paths meander through the trees making it a cool place to cycle round on warm summer days. (You can take up to four bikes on the metro – pay the child's fare for each and place them in one of the two bicycle carriages.)

30 Gijsbrecht van Aemstelpark

The park lies between Buitenvelderstelaan and van Leijenberghlaan **Free**
Open all hours **Metro** 51 to A.J. Ernstraat
The paths are wheelchair accessible

This unusual park in Buitenveldert ('outer fields') is a narrow strip of green between two much larger and better-known parks. This means it tends to be a bit quieter and there are rarely more than two or three people walking their dogs here in the morning. Designed in the 'English landscape style', large trees border the path and there are ponds and a canal to the south. This is a perfect place to wander or cycle through, even in winter.

31 Wertheimpark

Entrance on the corner of Plantage Middenlaan and Hortusplantsoen, opposite the Hortus Botanicus **Free**
Open 9am to half an hour before sunset
Tram 9, 14 to Mr Visserplien **Metro** Waterlooplein
The park is wheelchair accessible

One of twenty-three city parks in Amsterdam, Wertheimpark is the oldest and was named after the 19th-century Jewish philanthropist Abraham Wertheim. This small public park is a welcome patch of green in the midst of picturesque city streets. To the right of the entrance is a glass sculpture laid on the earth – a monument designed by Jan Wolkers to commemorate those who lost their lives at Auschwitz. It is easy to identify the entrance to the park, as two winged sphinxes sit on top of the stone pillars holding up the ornate gates.

㉜ Sarphatipark

Entrance on Sarphatipark (a section of Ceintuurbaan)
Free www.zuid.amsterdam.nl
Open all day, every day
Tram 3 to Sarphatipark or 16, 24 to Ceintuurbaan
The park has wide paths suitable for wheelchairs

Surrounded by grand 19th-century houses, Sarphatipark is a green haven in the midst of De Pijp, an area renowned for its busy market and lively mix of shops and restaurants. Built around one hundred and fifty years ago, the park was named after Samuel Sarphati, a city benefactor and doctor whose bust can be seen in an ornate memorial and fountain in the centre of the park. Although lots of people come to lie on the grass in the summer, there are secluded tree-lined paths on the fringes of the park and a quiet pond near to the Eerste van Sweelinckstraat entrance.

From Monday to Thursday the 'Groen Gemaal ', a plant and seed swap scheme, takes place in the park (for more information call (020) 664 1350).

33 Frankendael Park

Middenweg 72
Free www.park-frankendael.nl and www.restaurantmerkelbach.nl
Open all day, every day **Tram** 9 to the junction of Middenweg and Hugo de Vrieslaan
The park is accessible but the garden paths behind Frankendael House are covered in a thick layer of gravel

Many wealthy Amsterdammers wanted to live in attractive country retreats in the 18th century and Frankendael House is a magnificent example of such a property. Behind the private residence there's also a pretty formal garden with cherry blossom trees, red Fritillaria imperialis, white painted benches and low box hedges. Beyond this are 7 hectares of rather flat parkland, but one interesting feature is the brick-built chimney for nesting storks. In addition, the wooded area behind the house feels like a secret, overgrown and enticing place to wander. Ornate ironwork bridges cross small streams whilst above, vivid green parakeets perch on the branches of pine trees.

Cafe Merkelbach inside the former coach house of Frankendael Villa plays music, so find a table overlooking the exquisite formal garden if you prefer quietness.

34 Rozenoordpad

Turn west after Amsteldijk 273 to Rozenoordpad **Free**
Open all hours
Metro 50 or 52 to RAI station, then follow the pedestrian underpass away from the RAI Convention Centre
The cycle path is wheelchair accessible but is steep up the small hill

On the map it looks as if this path is very close to the A1 ring road, but surprisingly, the traffic isn't that audible. In summer the grass verges are transformed into a wonderful meadow, with poppies, cornflowers and foxgloves amongst the tall grasses. In winter this is also a good place to walk when the dykes are frozen over and there are clear views of the River Amstel below. At the corner of two canals is a mysterious large black and white sculpture of a man at a table wearing a dinner jacket.

Places to relax

35 Spa Zuiver

Koenenkade 8 ☎ (020) 301 0710
€ www.spazuiver.nl
Open every day from 10am–midnight
Bus 170, 172 to Koenenkade, 62 to Van den Boechorststraat
There is a lift to the changing rooms and pool but not all of the saunas are accessible for wheelchair users

Architecturally, this large, 3,000m² spa appears to be a modern interpretation of an ancient Roman baths, with its dark grey stone and vivid turquoise tiling. At its centre is an impressive rectangular warm pool where bathers can swim from inside into the enticing garden. Outdoors, there are numerous saunas, including the 'open hearth' which has a real fire inside a pine-infused log cabin. In summer, wander past fig trees and lavender bushes on your way to the outdoor hot tub, and in winter immerse yourself in the gurgling sunken aroma baths. Take your own dressing gown, flip flops and towels, otherwise these are added to the cost of your visit.

Throughout the year, 'badkleding' (swimsuit) days are on Tuesdays but at most other times nakedness is strictly enforced.

36 Koan Float

Float and Massage Centre, Herengracht 321
☎ (020) 555 0333
€ www.koanfloat.nl
Open every day 9am–11pm **Tram** 1,2, 5 to Spui
The centre is accessible for wheelchair users

According to enthusiasts, an hour of floating in a quiet, warm enclosed space is more relaxing than even a short nap. Apparently, tired muscles relax more easily when they are suspended in water (and Epsom salts are added to give extra buoyancy). This is a welcoming place to unwind with either a massage or gently recuperating in an almost soundproof flotation tank.

37 Sai Mithra Yogacentrum

St Antoniesbreestraat 102 ☎ (020) 636 2044
€ www.saimithra.nl
Open only during classes, see website for timetable
Metro Nieuwmarkt
There is wheelchair access but no specially adapted toilet

In the midst of the busy Antoniebreestraat, the Sai Mithra Centre offers a form of gentle, meditative yoga suited to people who want to find a sense of calm in their lives. Classes are in Dutch, but it is easy for non-native speakers to learn the basic terms and adopt the poses. In addition, intensive classes are held at weekends and there is a class for pregnant women on Friday afternoons.

38 Cosmetics and Care

Herenstraat 30a ☎ (020) 627 6732
€ www.cosmeticsandcare.com
Open Tuesday 10am–8pm, Wednesday, Friday, Saturday 10am–6pm, Thursday 10am–9pm
Tram 1, 2, 5, 13, 17 to Nieuwzijdskolk
Cosmetics and Care is on the ground floor but the toilet (in the basement) is not wheelchair accessible

Cosmetics and Care is one of the most relaxing places in Amsterdam to be offered massages and beauty advice.
The space is well designed with a living wall of plants by the entrance and felt and silk wall hangings by artist
Claudy Jongstra. Even the raw steel frames surrounding the glass-walled treatment rooms are polished with beeswax.
Although this attractive beauty parlour plays music, it's barely audible and the staff are so kind and attentive,
you hardly notice. In addition to offering pedicures, manicures and organic hair treatments this is also a restful place
to buy Dr Baumann facial care products and Valeur Absolue eau de parfum.

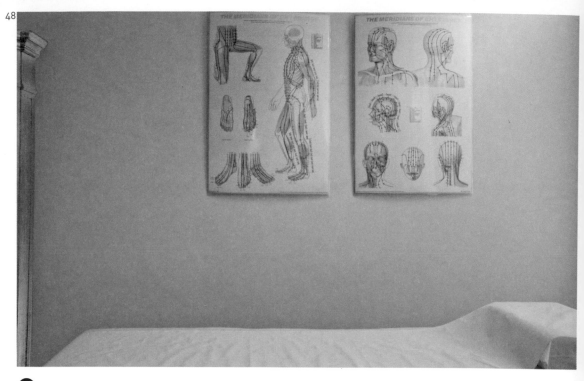

39 Oosterpark Acupuncture Practice

Oosterpark 84 ☎ (020) 421 6942
€ www.acupunctuur-welzijn.nl/en-index.htm
Open Appointments can be made between 9am–5pm, call well in advance as it is usually very booked up, no practice on Wednesday
Tram 3, 7, 9 or **Bus** 22, 37, 41 to Wijttenbachstraat
The practice is wheelchair accessible except for the small toilet

Gerrie Sporken has been running her traditional acupuncture practice for over twenty-five years and is very much admired by her patients. Situated on the edge of Oosterpark, the calm atmosphere of the treatment rooms is beneficial in itself. In additional to acupuncture, moxabustion is also used to treat various ailments. Her philosophy is to try to 'heal the spirit' as this often helps eliminate physical complaints.

40 Massage, Nicky van den Berg

Yoga Lifestyle Studio, Groenburgwal 9g ☎ (0) 640 581458 or (020) 663 1168
€ www.lifestylestudio.nl
Open Massage times are Wednesday 2pm–5.30pm, Friday 2pm–7pm and every other Saturday
Metro 51 or **Tram** 9, 14 to Waterlooplein or 9, 14, 24 to Muntplein (a 5-minute walk from either stop)
The Yoga Lifestyle Studio is not accessible for wheelchair users

Nicky van den Berg offers one of the best massages in Amsterdam. Anyone with tired shoulders or a stiff back not only gets deep tissue massage to relieve aches and pains, but she also introduces clients to the 'dolphin', a small hand held implement which deeply vibrates tense muscles. She also offers foot reflexology which helps to relax and heal the entire body. If you prefer to have a massage in silence, the gentle music with birdsong can be turned off at any time.

Places of worship

41 St Lucas Andreas Hospital Chapel

Jan Toroopstraat 164 ☎ (020) 510 8911
Free www.sintlucasandreasziekenhuis.nl
Open every day, time for prayer on Monday 12pm
Metro 50 to Jan van Galenstraat **Bus** 18, 64
Tram 13 to Jan Toroopstraat
The hospital and the chapel are wheelchair accessible

This large hospital on the west of the city not only has an impressive chapel but also a small adjoining 'quiet room'. The chapel is worth visiting for its stained glass windows which combine angular crosses and circular forms in mainly vivid ultramarine. Weekly services are held in the large space but the small quiet room next door has low level lighting and feels more private. In this room there is a bronze sculpture of a large, frayed book and a stone abstract piece underneath three semi-abstract etchings. There's also a book for people to write down their thoughts and two simple chairs. If needed, the chaplains can be contacted in their offices on the first floor of the hospital.

42 AMC Stiltecentrum

Academic Medical Centre, University of
Amsterdam, Meibergdreef 9 ☎ (020) 566 9111
(general information line for the AMC)
Free www.amc.nl
Open Services are held on Sunday mornings
10.30am–11.30am. Members of a spiritual care
team with humanistic, Christian and Islamic
backgrounds are available for advice and
support from Monday–Friday 9am–5pm
Metro 50, 54 to Holendrecht
The AMC is wheelchair accessible

The 'Stiltecentrum' (Quiet Centre) in this busy
teaching hospital welcomes anyone, whether they
are recovering from illness, work in the hospital
or are just looking for some quiet space. The main
room has an altar and sky blue floor-to-ceiling
panels held down with small pebbles. There
is also a small Russian Orthodox shrine and a
separate prayer room for Muslims.

43 Schiphol Airport Meditation Room

Vertrekpassage 219 ☎ (020) 601 4751
Free with a valid ticket to fly to or from Schiphol
Airport as the Meditation Room is beyond the
security checkpoint
www.luchthavenpastoraat.nl
Open daily 6am–11pm
Bus 197, 370 **Train** to Schiphol runs every 15
minutes from Central Station
The Meditation Centre is wheelchair accessible

This modern, glass-walled meditation centre
has three rooms: a quiet space for prayer or
meditation, a small library with a selection of
books and a meeting room where visitors can
make an appointment to see someone from the
pastoral centre. This is an enticing, well designed
space and a welcome contrast to the anonymity
of the airport. The meditation room is clearly
signposted and is located on the second floor
between E and F piers in lounge 43. It is easy to
recognise: the interior walls are decorated with
sandblasted figures of people praying, while above
there are inspiring curved 'sails' which point
towards the sky.

44 Oudekerk

Oudekerksplein 23 ☎ (020) 625 8284
€ www.oudekerk.nl
Open Monday–Saturday 11am–5pm, Sunday 1pm–5pm
Tram 4, 9, 16, 24, 25 to Dam or a 10-minute walk from Central Station
The building is wheelchair accessible

The Oudekerk or 'Old Church' was built in 1620 and was a very rowdy place in the 16th century as prostitutes and beggars mingled with devout pilgrims. It is now much more sedate and a very impressive building to walk around. The oak carvings of parables under the choir stalls are fascinating. You might find the half-man, half-chicken and the grotesque face with three eyes and two noses.

㊺ Oosterkerk

Kleine Wittenburgerstraat 1 ☎ (020) 627 2280
Free www.oosterkerk-amsterdam.nl **Open** daily from
9am–3pm for exhibitions, call for access at other times
Bus 22, 42, 43 to Kattenburgerplain
The building is wheelchair accessible and has a toilet for
people with disabilities

The Oosterkerk was constructed between 1669 and 1671
and is a significant landmark on the eastern edge of the
city centre. It's no longer used for religious services but
exhibitions of work by local artists are held here in the grand
but light filled interior. There are interesting star shaped
street designs in the courtyard in front of the main entrance.

㊻ Christ Church

Groenburgwal 42 ☎ (020) 624 8877
Free www.christchurch.nl
Open Services are held on Sundays at 10am **Tram** 4, 9,
14, 16, 19, 24, 25 to Muntplein or 9, 14 to Rembrandtplein
The church is accessable but the toilets are not adapted

Situated on a quiet street overlooking a canal, this
180-year-old Anglican church is a fine example of
Georgian Gothic. When Hans Christian Andersen attended
services during a visit to Amsterdam in 1866 he described
the church as 'small, intimate and well kept', and this
still holds true. Services are held in English, but you can
make an appointment to visit at other, quieter, times.

47 Ignatiushuis

Beulingstraat 11 ☎ (020) 679 8207
Free www.ignatiushuis.nl **Open** Monday–Friday 9.30am–
4.30pm, meditation Tuesday 10.30am–11.30am except July
and August when everyone is on retreat in the French
Alps **Tram** 1, 2, 5 to Koningsplein or Spui
There is no wheelchair access

Saint Ignatius House not only has a small art gallery on
the ground floor but also a lovely, simply furnished room
for meditation in the attic. This is a beautifully restored
space right in the centre of Amsterdam. You don't have to
be a Catholic to attend their Tuesday morning meditation
hour or many of their short courses.

48 Allemanskapel van St Joris

Oudezijds Achterburgwal 100 ☎ (020) 626 6634 **Free**
www.oudezijds100.nl/onze-inspiratie/allemanskapel.html
Open Prayers are held at 8.45am and 7.30pm, but
in-between these times, the chapel is open to visitors
for quiet contemplation **Tram** 51, 53, 54 to Nieuwmarkt
There is wheelchair access to the building

This chapel opens its doors to anyone looking for a peaceful
place, whether local office workers or tired tourists wanting
to recuperate from the excesses of the Red Light district.
The chapel consists of a simple room on the ground floor of
an old house. The sound of water trickling though the stone
channels invites calm reflection in this tranquil space.

49 Quaker Meeting House (Society of Friends)

Vossiusstraat 20 ☎ (020) 679 4238
Free www.quakers.nu
Open Meetings for worship are held on Sundays at 10.30am
Tram 2, 5 or **Bus** 170, 172 to the Rijksmuseum
The building is not wheelchair accessible

Once a week, anyone can attend the hour long, mainly silent meeting for worship. Quakers believe that there is something of God in everybody. Unlike many church services, there is no liturgy or priest but occasionally someone may 'bear witness' and say something thoughtful. Otherwise, as the building overlooks the Vondelpark, birdsong is usually the only sound you will hear. Coffee and herbal tea are served after the silence.

50 The Fo Guang Shan He Hua Temple, Zeedijk Buddhist Shambala

Meditation Centre, Zeedijk 8 ☎ (020) 420 2357
Free but donations are encouraged
www.ibps.nl/en/hehuatempel.htm
Open Monday–Saturday 12pm– 5pm, Sunday 10am–5pm
Metro Nieuwmarkt
There is no access for wheelchair users

Nuns from the Taiwanese Fo Kuangshan order invite people to visit their meditation room in the busy Chinatown district of Amsterdam. Surrounded by slightly scruffy South East Asian restaurants, the ornate yellow tiled roof of the temple looks extraordinary. Inside, the colour red dominates, however, as this is meant to bring good fortune in China. The followers of Fo Kuangshan are an order of Buddhists who try to implement their beliefs in everyday life and there is copious information about the temple and Buddhism in English on their webpage.

51 European Zen Centre Amsterdam

Valckenierstraat 35 ☎ (020) 625 8884
€ except for free introductory classes on Sunday at 10.30am
www.zen-deshimaru.nl
Open Classes are held Tuesday–Thursday 7.30am–9am, Friday 7am, Tuesday and Thursday 6.30pm–8pm,
Saturday 10am, Sunday 11am
Tram 7, 10 to Weesperstraat or K's-Gravesandestraat
The dojo is wheelchair accessible but the toilets have narrow doors

Located in a quiet backstreet near Amsterdam University, this welcoming Zen centre has a large dojo (meditation room)
for zazen, the Zen name for silent meditation. Introductory classes are held on Sunday mornings and the centre also
arranges zazen weekends around every two months and month-long courses in Spain and other countries. Classes are
taught in Dutch but some teachers may explain terms in English if a few non-Dutch speakers turn up.

52 Amstelkerk

Amstelveld 10 ☎ (020) 520 0070 **Free**
Open During exhibitions the church is open from 9am–5pm
Tram 4, 16, 24, 25 to Keizersgracht, then walk eastwards down Kerkstraat
The church is wheelchair accessible

This handsome wooden church was originally built as a temporary structure but it has survived here since the 17th century. Although part of the building has been converted into a restaurant and the office for urban regeneration, the interior is still well worth seeing. The nave is square rather than the usual elongated rectangle and if you look up, you can read Dutch inscriptions painted on the walls. Art exhibitions are often held here, giving locals and visitors the opportunity to spend some time in this interesting church.

53 H.H. Petrus en Pauluskerk (Papegaai)

Kalverstraat 58 ☎ (020) 623 1889
Free www.nicolaas-parochie.nl/
papegaaiamsterdam.html
Open daily 10am–4pm except on
Sunday and during services
Tram 4, 9, 16, 24, 25 to Dam or Rokin
The church is wheelchair accessible

Named after the carved stone parrot
on the exterior façade ('papegaai' is
Dutch for parrot), this 19th-century
church was built on what has since
become one of the busiest shopping
streets in the Netherlands. It can
get very crowded in Kalverstraat,
especially at weekends, so if you want
some respite from noisy shop music,
the Papegaai Church is open most of
the day.

54 St Nicolaaskerk

Prins Hendrikkade 73 ☎ (020) 624 8749
Free www.nicolaas-parochie.nl
Open Monday, Saturday 12pm–3pm, Tuesday–Friday 11am–4pm, unless services are being held, such as the 'silent mass held at 12.30pm Monday–Saturday (in Spanish on Fridays)
Bus 22, 43, 42 or **Tram** 1, 2, 4, 9, 13, 24, 26 or **Metro** to Central Station
Wheelchair users can inform a member of staff to gain access to the church via a lift

The interior of this magnificent Neo-Baroque Catholic church may not to be everyone's taste, but it is one of the more visited churches in Amsterdam due to its central location. The interior is a rather strange combination of grey plaster and ornate mouldings which was considered unusual in 1887 when it was built. The church lies opposite Central Station and is a quiet oasis in the midst of a busy thoroughfare. To avoid seeing the church during choral events, check concert times on their website.

55 Portuguese Synagogue

Mr L.E. Visserplein 3 ☎ (020) 624 5351
€ except during services
www.esnoga.com
Open April–October Sunday–Friday 10am–4pm; November–March Tuesday–Thursday 10am–4pm, Friday 10am–2pm
Tram 9, 14 to Meneer Visserplein **Metro** Waterlooplein
The synagogue is wheelchair accessible

Once a year, this gorgeous building is lit with hundreds of candles for 'Museum Night', an annual event in early November when around thirty-five museums open their doors until the early hours of the morning. At other times it is worth visiting to learn about Jewish religious observance and see the beautiful interior with its wooden pews, brass chandeliers and elegant pillars.

56 Thomaskerk

Prinses Irenesraat 36 ☎ (020) 673 9230 or (020) 662 5170 for the quiet chapel
Free www.thomaskerk.nl
Open The quiet hour in the chapel is Monday–Friday 12.30pm–1.30pm
Metro Zuid **Tram** 5 **Bus** 65 to Prinses Irenestraat
The church and chapel are wheelchair accessible

From the outside, the Thomaskerk looks rather ordinary and uninspiring but don't let this deter you from visiting. Once inside, the interior is quite astounding. Inspired by the idea of Jesus in the desert, the church roof was designed in the shape of a huge tent. Sand coloured, rough concrete walls are simple and unadorned, and the small windows allow light to fall in straight beams on to the altar at certain times of the day. There is also a small, beautiful chapel (the 'stiltekapel') at the rear of the building, where a lunchtime meditation hour is held on weekdays. Only a few minutes' walk from the World Trade Centre, this is the perfect place to spend some quiet time.

57 Onze Lieve Gasthuis Chapel

Oosterpark 9 ☎. (020) 599 2494
Free www.olvg.nl **Open** daily 10am–5pm **Tram** 3, 7 to Beukenweg or 3 to Camperstraat **Bus** 37 to Beukenplein **Metro** 51, 53, 54 to Weesperstraat or Wibautstraat
The entire building is wheelchair accessible

This modern hospital on the eastern edge of the city has some stunning sculptures in the 'lichthal' (light hall), an inviting, glass-roofed walkway through the outpatients area. The most architecturally impressive part of the building, however, is the recently built chapel. Based on a Romanesque design, the simple interior exudes a sense of stillness and calm.

58 Vredeskerk

Vredeskerkplein 1 ☎ (020) 662 6909
Free www.amsterdam.vredeskerk.nl **Open** The Eucharist is held every day at 12.30pm, a children's service is on Saturday at 6.30pm **Tram** 12, 25 to Cornelis Troostplein
The church is accessible for wheelchair users

Dating from 1918, the dark interior of this large church seems to be a combination of Neo-Gothic and the Amsterdam School style of architecture and includes a floor covered in ornate tilework. This is a busy parish building, but it is often open for quiet reflection during the day. Even if the church is closed, the beautiful sculptures in the small square outside the church are worth seeing.

Small shops

⁵⁹ Pop𝖆rt Antique Toys

Kerkstraat 215 ☎ (020) 427 8524
www.antiquetoys.nl
Open by appointment
Tram 4, 16, 24, 25 to Keizersgracht
The small shop is not wheelchair accessible but everything is
visible from the window and the owner can take anything off the
shelves for customers

Claartje Pennink specialises in antique toys and this beautiful
shop is like a perfect miniature museum, but with the added
attraction that everything is for sale. You'll find 19th-century paper
toys such as tiny peepshows, numerous board games, wooden
toys and folk art. On the shelves sit wide-eyed, wooden limbed
Pennsylvania Dutch Dolls, next to a paddling of tinplate ducks
and their yellow ducklings.

60 Zonnemeer

Nieuwe Kerkstraat 8 ☎ (020) 625 1223
www.zonnemeer.nl **Open** Monday–Friday 8.30am–
6.30pm, Saturday 8.30am–5pm
Tram 9, 14, 7, 10 to Waterlooplein **Metro** Waterlooplein
The shop is wheelchair accessible but very small

A delightful small shop near to the Amstel, full of fresh
organic vegetables, wines, bread, cheeses, yoghurts and
natural beauty products. The two women who work here
are friendly and soon recognise regular shoppers. You
can also order a weekly bag of fruit and vegetables direct
from Dutch farmers. Try Zonnemeer's specialities; fresh
kalamata olives from the tub or sauerkraut soaked in brine.

61 Paul Année Bakery

Runstraat 25 ☎ (020) 623 5322
www.de9straatjes.nl/nl/winkels/?shopid=126187
Open Monday–Friday 8am–6pm, Saturday 8.30am–5pm
Tram 7, 10, 17 to Elandsgracht
Stairs make entry for wheelchair users difficult

This Dutch bakery is renowned for its wholemeal bread,
ginger cakes and raisin biscuits. Everything is baked on
the premises. Pick up a slice of rosemary covered foccacia
bread for lunch, or try their 'appeltassen' (apple in pastry)
– a perfect tea-time treat while cycling alongside canals.
Look out for the sculptures in the window made from the
shop's distinctive green and white striped paper bags.

62 De Aanzet

Frans Halsstraat 27 ☎ (020) 673 3415
www.de-aanzet.nl
Open Monday–Friday 9am–6pm, Saturday 9am–5pm
Tram 16, 24, 25 to Heinekenplein
The shop is wheelchair accessible

This rustic organic food shop is a wonderful emporium for both healthy eaters and gourmets. Not only do they have an interior 'market stall' of boxes filled to the brim with fresh fruit and a huge variety of familiar and unusual vegetables, but also a wide selection of organic cheeses and fresh bread. At the back of the shop you'll also find a shelf of natural household paints made of linseed oil, and environmentally friendly cleaning materials.

63 Art and Flowers

KNSM Laan 6 ☎ (020) 419 2273
www.artandflowers.nl
Open Monday 10am–1pm, Tuesday–Friday 10am–6pm, Saturday 10am–5pm
Tram 10 or **Bus** 42, 65 to Azartplein
The shop is wheelchair accessible

Walking into this sophisticated florists is a bit like entering a stunning art gallery. The strong colours of crimson and purple flowers alongside emerald green leaves and striking vertical arrangements of twigs and tall blooms make this a spectacular shop to wander round. Their abstract Japanese influenced designs often include driftwood or aloe vera stalks tucked inside a nest of prickly cacti. Art and Flowers also make exquisite bridal bouquets and stunning displays for the urban garden.

64 Jacob Hooy Apothecary

Kloveniersburgwal 10–12 ☎ (020) 624 3041
www.jacob-hooy.nl
Open Wednesday 1pm–5pm, Thursday–Saturday 11am–5pm and by appointment
Metro to Nieuwmarkt or a 12-minute walk from Central Station
The shop is wheelchair accessible but is rather cramped inside

This wonderful old apothecary has been selling herbs and spices from the Far East since 1743. The numerous shelves still have their old wooden drawers with Latin inscriptions, although you can also now get modern salves, creams, juices, herbal tea, and other health foods here. This is an excellent place to buy liquorice from the jar, which is then weighed and wrapped up in triangular brown paper bags. In the room on the right you'll also find hundreds of jars of vitamins as well as Weleda natural cosmetics.

65 Tinctoria

Zanddwarsstraat 9 ☎ (020) 623 8008 www.tinctoria.nl
Open Wednesday 1.30pm–6pm, Thursday, Friday 10am–
6pm, Saturday 2pm–5pm **Metro** to Nieuwmarkt
The shop is wheelchair accessible but quite small

The name Tinctoria hints at what goes on behind the
scenes in this small, delightful shop. The owner uses the
surprisingly intense hues of madder and other natural
dyes to transform beautiful silk viscose velvet into elegant
cushions, dressing gowns and scarves. Everything is sewn
on the premises and as this is one of the quietest streets
in Amsterdam, this shop is a real treat for people who
want to avoid the crowds in department stores.

66 Gerda's Flowers

Runstraat 16 ☎ (020) 624 2912
www.theninestreets.com/gerda.html
Open Monday–Friday 9am–6pm, Saturday 9am–5pm
Tram 7, 10, 17 to Elandsgracht
The shop is wheelchair accessible but small and rather
crowded with flower displays

This lovely shop in the pretty 'nine streets' area has an
extraordinary array of plants and flowers. Their floral
arrangements adorn handsome canalside venues during
the annual Amsterdam Grachtenfestival. They specialise
in creating elegant orchid arrangements and sell
spectacular hand-made vases by contemporary designers.

⁶⁷ Le Fournil

Olympiaplein 119 ☎ (020) 672 4211
www.lefournil.nl
Open Monday–Saturday 7am–7pm ·
Tram 24 or **Bus** 15 to Olympiaplein
The small shop has a ramp but it may be difficult to turn round in a wheelchair

Join the expectant queue outside to sample some of the most delicious bread in the Netherlands. This French bakery is incredibly popular, not only for their four different kinds of baguettes (including one covered in poppy seeds), but also for their hazelnut biscuits and regionally sourced honey. Their chausson aux pommes are a delectable reminder of Parisien patisseries. You can even take home a few of the madelaines that so inspired Proust.

Restaurants and cafes

68 De Pilsener Club

Begijnesteeg 4 ☎ (020) 623 1777
Open Monday–Thursday 12pm–1am, Friday, Saturday 12pm–2am, closed Sunday and bank holidays
Tram 1, 2, 5, 9, 14, 16, 25 to Spui then a few minutes' walk to the right of the Beguinehof
The toilets are on the ground floor but are not accessible for wheelchair users as they are very narrow

Don't be put off by its name, this small cafe is open to everyone and you don't even have to drink pils. Known locally as the English Ass, De Pilsener Club is one of Amsterdam's traditional 'brown bars'. It is 115 years old and has been owned by the same family since the 1920s. Entering, it's like discovering a tiny museum cafe with the current owner's grandfather's paintings on the nicotine-brown walls. Tucked down a backstreet behind a busy shopping area, it's the perfect place to enjoy one of their 16 bottled or 5 draught beers. Unusually, there's no bar counter, but the staff is so attentive, you don't even notice. This cafe is living proof that quietness and happiness are totally compatible – and this isn't just down to sipping a couple of their distinctive Dutch jenevers.

69 Cafe-Restaurant Dauphine

Prins Bernhardplein 175 ☎ (020) 462 1646
www.caferestaurantdauphine.nl
Open Monday–Thursday, Saturday, Sunday 9am–1am, Friday 9am–2am
Tram 12 or **Metro** to Amstel
Wheelchair accessible, but call ahead if you are using their car park so you can get access to the lift

This huge restaurant used to be a car showroom, but this is hard to imagine now as the contemporary interior design is both sophisticated and enticing. Huge glass lampshades hang over the bar and the tables and chairs are a dramatic brown and red – a typical Dutch combination of sober and vibrant colours. Despite filling up most evenings, other people's conversations remain unobtrusive and there probably won't be many tourists here as the restaurant is a metro ride from the centre. Instead, you'll find mainly Amsterdammers enjoying good food and conversation. Their menu includes grilled halibut on layers of spinach and fennel, pasta with clams and surprisingly tasty deep-fried soft shell crabs.

70 Pompadour

Kerkstraat 148 ☎ (020) 330 0981

www.iens.nl/restaurant/17686/amsterdam-pompadour

Open Monday–Friday 11.30am–4pm, Saturday 11.30am–5pm, Sunday 12pm–4pm

Tram 4, 16, 24, 25 to Keizersgracht or 3, 7, 10, 12 to Spiegelgracht

Pompadour is not wheelchair accessible as there are two steps into the cafe.

This excellent patisserie is one of two small cafes which also produce their own exquisite chocolate and pastries. The interior design is stylish yet simple with dark brown leather seating and cherry wood panelling, making this one of the most sophisticated tea rooms in the Netherlands. The main attraction, however, is the food. Chef Escu Gabriels' plate of delicious grilled vegetables is one of the best lunches to be had in the city.

(71) In de Waag

Nieuwmarkt 4 ☎ (020) 422 7772
www.indewaag.nl
Open daily 9am–10.30pm (lunch from 10am–4pm)
Metro 51, 53, 54 to Nieuwmarkt
The building is accessible for wheelchair users and has a specially adapted toilet

This atmospheric building is one of the most impressive medieval structures still standing in Amsterdam. Lit by over two hundred flickering candles in cast iron candelabras, this former weighing house built in 1488 is now a thriving restaurant. The terrace can get crowded in summer, so have a fresh mint tea inside if it seems busy outdoors.

72 In de Wildeman

Kolksteeg 3 ☎ (020) 638 2348
www.indewildeman.nl
Open Monday–Thursday 12pm–1am, Friday, Saturday 12pm–2am, closed on Sunday
Tram 1, 2, 5, 13, 17 to Nieuwzijdskolk or a 10-minute walk from Central Station
The bar is accessible but the toilets are down a flight of steps

This traditional Amsterdam cafe is a mecca for European beer drinkers. With eighteen beers on draught and over two hundred and fifty bottled ales, deciding what to drink isn't always easy. As well as the local organic Zatte and Natte from Brouwerij t'IJ (locally brewed in a windmill), you'll also find unusual Belgian beers such as Mort Subite, which continues to ferment after bottling. There are even a few English names, including Wychwood's Fiddler's Elbow but just one beer from France; the intriguingly named Belzebuth.

73 Nam-Kee Nieuwmarkt

Geldersekade 117 ☎ (020) 639 2848
www.namkee.net **Open** Monday–Friday 4pm–12am,
Saturday, Sunday 2.30pm–12am, closes early on New
Year's Eve **Metro** Nieuwmarkt or a 10-minute walk
from Central Station
The restaurant is not wheelchair accessible

Delicious food, fast service . . . what more could anyone
want from a Chinese restaurant? This is one of the best
places to eat around Nieuwmarkt; Amsterdam's very own
Chinatown. It does get busy so you may have to queue at
peak times, but it is well worth the wait. You could also
try their sister restaurant in Zeedijk.

74 Albina

Albert Cuypstraat 69 ☎ (020) 675 5135
Open Tuesday–Saturday 10.30am–10pm, Sunday 12pm–
10pm, closed Monday **Tram** 16, 24 to Albert Cuypmarkt
The restaurant is on the ground floor but the toilet has a
narrow door

Near to the bustling Albert Cuypmarkt, this relaxed and
informal cafe offers cheap but tasty Surinamese dishes
to the locals. This is one of the few places where fast
food is consistently nourishing and very filling. Try the
rotis (wheat and lentil pancake-type breads), which come
with a curry sauce, potatoes, green beans and meat or
vegetables.

75 Cafe in the Tassenmuseum Hendrikje

Herengracht 573 ☎ (020) 524 6452
www.tassenmuseum.nl/en/your-visit/museum-cafe
Open every day 10am–5pm, closed Christmas Day, New
Year's Day, 30 April, early closing on 24 and 31 December
Tram 9, 14 to Rembrantplein
Most of the building is wheelchair accessible

This impressive museum on the stately Herengracht shows
the world's largest collection of bags and purses. Although
the main exhibition spaces can get crowded at weekends,
the cafe seems to offer quiet repose. Sit in sumptuous
velvet covered chairs in an elegant drawing room or retire
to the airy conservatory overlooking the small garden.

76 Nieuwe Kafe

Eggertstraat 8 ☎ (020) 627 2830
www.nieuwe-kafe.nl **Open** daily 10am–6pm
Tram 4, 9, 16, 24, 25 or 1, 2, 5, 13, 14, 17 to Dam
The cafe has good access for people with mobility problems

This cafe was converted from part of the Nieuwe Kerk
(New Church) and is an ideal place to sit after visiting an
exhibition, as well for shoppers in the busy streets nearby.
Avoid sitting on the outdoor terrace overlooking Dam
Square if you want to steer clear of the crowds and the
occasional noisy funfair. Their coffee is good, however,
so if you are looking for somewhere central to recuperate
from busy streets, this cafe is a good location.

77 Brasserie Bark

Van Baerlestraat 120 ☎ (020) 675 0210
www.bark.nl
Open Monday–Friday 12pm–3pm and 5.30pm–12.30am, Saturday and Sunday 12pm–12.30am
Tram 5, 16 or **Bus** 142, 170 to Museumplein
The restaurant is wheelchair accessible

Bark's speciality is the chilled seafood platter which comes with small dangerous looking implements to winkle out the meat from lobster claws and other seemingly impenetrable crustacean cavities. Located near the Concertegebouw, this upmarket restaurant is an ideal place for a post-concert meal. The staff is welcoming and efficient which makes Bark even more reminiscent of a French brasserie. They are also open to midnight – one of the very few restaurants in the city to keep their kitchens open after 11pm.

78 Christophe

Leliegracht 46 ☎ (020) 625 08 07
www.restaurantchristophe.nl
Open Tuesday–Saturday 6.30pm–10.30pm, closed Sunday and Monday
Tram 13, 14, 17 to Westermarkt
The restaurant has a ground floor dining area but the toilets are down a flight of steps so are unsuitable for wheelchair users

Beautifully decorated with subtly coloured photos of gourmet dishes on the wall, this sophisticated restaurant serves inventive and delicious food for discerning diners. They never play music so this remains one of the few quiet spots by the entrancing inner city canals. Overall, this is a very civilised place to dine with someone close or with friends.

⑦⑨ Brasserie Flo

Amstelstraat 9 ☎ (020) 8904757
www.floamsterdam.com
Open Tuesday–Friday 12pm–3pm and every day 5.30pm–12am
Tram 9, 14 to Rembrandtplein
The restaurant is wheelchair accessible

This sophisticated yet welcoming brasserie is renowned for its fruits de mer and their fresh crab is the highlight of their copious seafood platters. With its Belle Epoque wall paintings and handsome brass bar rails, dining here feels like being in early 20th-century Paris. Their pan-fried scallops with a ragout of artichokes, fried girolle mushrooms and truffle sauce is a particularly nice dish, as is their cherry clafoutis with kirsch sabayon and cinnamon ice-cream. Brasserie Flo's wine selection is superb and this is definitely a place to linger when the skies outside are grey.

80 Cafe Restaurant Amsterdam

Watertorenplein 6 ☎ (020) 682 2666
www.cradam.nl **Open** daily 10.30am–12am, Friday and
Saturday until 1am. The kitchen is open daily 10.30am–
10.30pm, Friday and Saturday until 11.30pm
Tram 10 to Van Hallstraat **Bus** 22 to Van der Hoopstraat
The restaurant and bar are wheelchair accessible

The white linen tablecloths and simple décor make this an
enticing place to lunch alone or with friends. Even during
busy periods, the place is so huge that sound is dispersed
and you can easily converse with your fellow diners. This
magnificent industrial monument (a former water pumping
station) is also worth visiting for its seafood platters.

81 De Kas

Kamerlingh Onneslaan 3 ☎ (020) 462 4562
www.restaurantdekas.nl **Open** Monday–Friday
12pm–2pm and 6.30pm–10pm, Saturday 6.30pm–10pm
Bus 41, 357 or **Tram** 9 to Hogeweg
The restaurant is wheelchair accessible

De Kas used to be the city greenhouse, supplying
Amsterdam markets with fruit and vegetables. Most of the
produce used by chefs at De Kas is now grown in outlying
nurseries but a few edible flowers, herbs and vegetables
are still tended in close proximity to the kitchen. This is a
remarkable place to eat: the food is exceptional and the
light-filled restaurant feels spacious and open.

82 Marius

Barentszstraat 243 ☎ (020) 422 7880

Open Tuesday–Saturday 6.30pm–10pm, closed Sunday and Monday

Tram 3 to Houtmankade, Barendstzstraat is on the right, at the end of Plancuisstraat **Bus** 48 to Barendtzplein
The restaurant is on the ground floor but the toilet is rather small for wheelchair users

Marius is run by Kees Elfring, a dynamic, inventive chef who changes his menu according to what is in season.
This is one of the best restaurants in Amsterdam, the staff is welcoming and friendly and serve quite delicious food.
Situated in a non-touristy district of the city, the main room isn't too large so conversations don't get very loud.
The restaurant also has a glass roofed conservatory which is popular on summer evenings. Try their Grande
Bouillabaisse de Marcel Pagnal followed by a raspberry and almond tart with home-made vanilla ice-cream.

83 Zuid Zeeland

Herengracht 413 ☎ (020) 624 3154 www.zuidzeeland.nl
Open weekdays 12pm–2.30pm and Monday–Sunday
6pm–11pm **Tram** 1, 2, 5 to Koningsplein or Spui
The restaurant is wheelchair accessible

Dining at Zuid Zeeland is quite an experience. Offering
only one place setting each evening, the master chefs
conjure up some of the most exquisite 'slow food' you will
ever taste. Each dish, from the beautifully presented main
courses to the delicate amuses bouches, is a surprising
combination of ingredients, many of which you wouldn't
expect to find on the same plate. In summer, diners can
sit on the sunny terrace overlooking the quiet canal.

84 Beddington's

Utrechtsedwarsstraat 141 ☎ (020) 620 7393
www.beddington.nl **Open** Tuesday–Saturday from 7pm,
closed Sunday and Monday **Tram** 7, 10 to Oosteinde
Metro 51, 53, 54 to Weesperplein
Small wheelchairs can be accommodated

Run by the enterprising British chef Jean Beddington,
this small but elegant restaurant is one of the best in
Amsterdam. The interior design is impeccable and the chefs
serve consistently inventive, beautifully presented food. Try
her smoked salmon croquettes with yellow paprika, broccoli
and lime mayonnaise followed by a canele of black figs in
fennel caramel served with Guinness ice cream.

85 Felix Meritis

Keizersgracht 324 ☎ (020) 626 2321
www.felix.meritis.nl **Open** Monday–Friday 9am–7pm
Tram 13, 14, 17 to Westermarkt or 1, 2, 5, Spui
The cafe has a small ramp but the toilets are not
wheelchair accessible

Ever since it was built in 1787, Felix Meritis has been a
thriving cultural centre and continues to organise debates
on philosophy, science and the arts. This architecturally
impressive building also has a cafe on the ground floor,
serving tea, coffee and a small selection of beers, wines
and spirits. There is also a narrow outside terrace
overlooking the canal, a nice place to sit in sunny weather.

86 De Belhamel

Brouwersgracht 60 ☎ (020) 622 1095 www.belhamel.nl
Open every day 12pm–4pm and Monday–Thursday
6pm–10pm, Friday and Saturday 6pm–10.30pm **Bus** 18, 21,
22 to Singel or a 10-minute walk from Central Station
The outdoor terrace and ground floor seating are
wheelchair accessible but the first floor is not

Situated on the corner where the pretty Brouwersgracht
and Herengracht canals meet, this is one of the nicest
places to dine outdoors in Amsterdam. Not only is the
view from the terrace entrancing, the Art Nouveau interior
is also quite special. The food is also excellent, and they
were recently awarded a Michelen 'Bib Gourmand'.

87 Papeneiland Cafe

Prinsengracht 2 ☎ (020) 624 1989
www.papeneiland.nl
Open Monday–Thursday 11am–1am, Friday–Sunday 11am–2am
Bus 18, 21, 22 to Buiten Brouwersgracht
The cafe is not wheelchair accessible

This astonishing cafe, built in 1642, is not only renowned for its beautiful hand-painted Delft tiles, it also has an illustrious history. In the 17th century Dutch Catholics would escape their persecutors by fleeing in a secret tunnel underneath the bar. Nowadays, people come here for their delicious homemade apple pie or for lively conversation on the small terrace overlooking two canals. This is the ideal location to sample 20-year-old Dutch jenever, the locally brewed sprit from Distillery van Wees, the only distillery still left in Amsterdam. Look out for 'De Ooievaar' red seals on the brown stoneware bottles.

88 Cafe de Druif

Rapenburgerplein 83 ☎ (020) 624 4530
Open Monday–Thursday, Sunday 2.30pm–1am, Friday
and Saturday 2.30pm–2am **Bus** 22, 42, 42 to Kadijksplein
Tram 9, 14 to Mr Visserplein
The cafe is not wheelchair accessible

One of the oldest cafes in Amsterdam, dating from around
1630, De Druijf used to be a jenever distillery and the
barrels still hang above the bar. There's mainly Amstel
draught beer but you can also order other bottled ales.
This very traditional bar is friendly and informal. You won't
find three course meals here, however, only the owner's
home-cured eels and a few other typical Dutch snacks.

89 Puccini

Staalstraat 21 ☎ (020) 620 8458 www.puccini.nl
Open daily 8.30am–6pm, Saturday and Sunday 10am–
6pm, and until 8pm if there is a performance on at the
nearby Muziektheater and you reserve dinner in advance
Metro Waterlooplein **Tram** 9, 14 to Waterlooplein
Accessible for wheelchair users but the toilet is small

Sister to Puccini, the very sophisticated chocolate shop
next door, this small cafe close to the River Amstel is
a perfect place for lunch. The small terrace is a good
sun-trap in warm weather but even in winter it is worth
coming here to curl up indoors with a hot chocolate
and croissant.

90 Cafe VUMC

The cafe is inside the main Vrije Universiteit Medical Centrum (VUMC) on De Boelelaan

☎ (020) 444 4444 (main hospital switchboard)

Open Monday–Friday 8am–8.30pm, Saturday and Sunday 11am–10.30pm

Tram 16, 24 **Metro** 50, 51

The hospital is wheelchair accessible

This was a real surprise; hospital restaurants can be gloomy places but this is a light-filled, architecturally interesting place to have morning or afternoon tea. The smoked salmon or brie and walnut-filled bread rolls and coffee pastries make the menu rather limited but it's still a pleasant place to sit and talk.

Bookshops

Athenaeum Boekhandel

Spui 14–16 ☎ (020) 514 1460
www.athenaeum.nl
Open Monday 11am–6pm, Tuesday, Wednesday, Saturday 9.30am–6pm, Thursday 9.30am–9pm, Friday 9.30am–6.30pm, Sunday 12pm–5.30pm
Trams 1, 2, 4, 5, 9, 14, 16, 24, 25 to either Spui stop
Very limited access for wheelchair users, but their huge array of magazines can be browsed outside

Athenaeum bookshop has a huge collection of titles to choose from. Not only do they supply Amsterdam University departments, they also provide an excellent service for students and non-academics. They have over 50,000 titles in stock, from anthropology to ancient history, as well as the largest French department in the Netherlands. They even have a selection of mouth-watering cookery books and very eye-catching window displays. After a visit here, curious readers wander though the Friday book market on Spui, the cobbled square outside.

92 Boekie Woekie Books by Artists

Berenstraat 16 ☎ (020) 639 0507

http://boewoe.home.xs4all.nl

Open daily 12pm–6pm

Tram 13, 14, 17 to Westermarkt then a 10-minute walk down Prinsengracht

The shop can accommodate wheelchair users

Although this wonderful small shop describes itself as the place to find artist's books, it also stocks limited edition DVDs and audio recordings – most of which you won't find anywhere else. You'll discover strange and wonderful things here from *How to Draw a Bunny*, a film about a mischievous artist, to *In Every Picture*, Erik Kessels' engrossing anthologies of found photographs. Spend an afternoon browsing shelves full of idiosyncratic photobooks, artist's multiples and hand-printed ephemera. Every town in the world should have one of these bookshops – mainly because they value the intriguing things artists have made themselves. This is a wonderful place to discover the curious thoughts of a lone scribbler or some colourful screen-printed postcards.

93 Kirchner Boekhandel

Leliegracht 32 ☎ (020) 624 4449
www.boekhandelkirchner.com
Open Monday 1pm–6pm, Tuesday–Friday 9.30am–6pm, Saturday 9.30am–5pm
Tram 13, 14, 17 to Westermarkt
The shop can't really accommodate wheelchair users as narrow steps lead to other floors

This well-stocked bookshop overlooks one of the nicest canals in the city and is a real pleasure to visit. People who work here are knowledgeable as well as very helpful and will be able to direct you to a particular theologian or writer on religion. In amongst the numerous small alcoves you'll also find philosophy books, postcards of icons and even an illustrated guide to Venice and the Islamic world.

94 Mulder Boekhandel

Cornelis Schuystraat 14 ☎ (020) 662 5680
www.boekhandelmulder.nl
Open Monday 10am–6pm, Tuesday–Friday 9am–6pm, Saturday 9am–5pm
Tram 2 to Cornelis Schuystraat
Just the entrance and the magazine section of the shop is accessible for wheelchair users

This medium sized, independent bookshop has a wide range of titles and a few shelves of English fiction. Situated in the middle of a very well-to-do neighbourhood in Amsterdam, this is a quiet place to wander round and browse through some recent novels and children's books. The staff is helpful and welcoming and can order other titles if what you want isn't on the shelves.

95 Waterstones

Kalverstraat 152 ☎ (020) 638 3821
www.waterstones.com/waterstonesweb/home.do
Open Monday 10am–6pm, Tuesday, Wednesday, Friday
9.30am–6.30pm, Thursday 9.30am–9pm, Saturday
9.30am–7pm, Sunday 11am–6pm
Tram 1, 2, 4, 5, 9, 14, 16, 24, 25 to either Spui stop
Only the ground floor is accessible

Waterstones is one of the largest English language
bookshops in Amsterdam. It doesn't play taped music, so
is a quiet place to spend some time reading or browsing
in the city centre. Each department is clearly signposted
and there are enticing window seats on most floors.

96 Geografische Boekhandel Pied à Terre

Overtoom 135-137 ☎ (020) 627 4455 www.piedaterre.nl
or www.jvw.nl **Open** Monday 1pm–6pm, Tuesday,
Wednesday, Friday 10am–6pm, Thursday 10.00am–9pm,
Saturday 10am–5pm **Tram** 1, 3, 12 to Overtoom
The bookshop is wheelchair accessible, but not the toilets

This large bookshop used to be a theatre and there is
definitely something dramatic about the spacious interior.
This is one of the best-stocked travel bookshops in the
world and the staff is very knowledgeable. There are
innumerable guides to both local and far-flung places and
a great selection of globes. Hard to find maps of cycle and
walking routes are kept in wooden drawers on the balcony.

97 Selexyz Scheltema

Koningsplein 20 ☎ (020) 523 1411
www.selexyz.nl **Open** Monday–Wednesday, Friday,
Saturday 10am–7pm, Thursday 10am–9pm, Sunday
12pm–6pm **Tram** 1, 2, 5 stop nearby
Most of the shop is accessible by wheelchair

Although this huge bookshop has five floors and over
125,000 books, it is still a quiet place to browse. Most of
the building was constructed in the early part of the 20th
century and has a calm atmosphere, but in one corner on
the first floor there is also a small room with an original
17th-century plaster moulding on the ceiling. There are
hundreds of English language books on sale here.

98 Martyrium

van Baerlestraat 170 ☎ (020) 673 2092
www.hetmartyrium.nl
Open Monday–Friday 9am–6pm, Saturday 9am–5pm,
Sunday 12pm–5pm **Tram** 3, 5, 12, 24 to Roelof Hartplein
Some parts of the shop are wheelchair accessible

This bookshop is rather like a Tardis; from the outside
it looks rather small but the interior is actually very
spacious. Composed of two levels, Martyrium is an ideal
place to find books about Amsterdam and the Netherlands
The bookshop staff have their own specialist interests, so
even if you don't see exactly what you're looking for on the
shelves, they'll try to find other titles for you.

99 De Dolfijn

Haarlemmerdijk 92 ☎ (020) 422 3945
http://boekhandeldedolfijn.nl
Open Monday 11am–6.30pm, Tuesday–Friday 9.30am–6.30pm, Saturday 9.30am–6pm
Tram 3 to Harlemmerplein **Bus** 18, 21, 22, 348, 353 to Buiten Oranjestraat
The bookshop has a small step at the entrance but is otherwise accessible

This medium-sized independent bookshop mainly stocks Dutch titles and is renowned for its wide selection of contemporary novels. Travel books are easy to find at the front of the shop and the children's section at the rear is very inviting. One of the few bookshops to open a bit later on weekdays and on Saturdays, this is a good place to find a last-minute present.

🕙 **100 Pantheon**

St. Antoniesbreestraat 132-134 ☎ (020) 622 9488
www.pantheonboekhandel.nl
Open Monday 12pm–6pm, Tuesday–Friday 9am–6pm, Saturday 9am–5pm, Sunday 12pm–5pm
Metro 51, 53, 54 to Nieuwmarkt or a 12-minute walk from Central Station
The shop can accommodate wheelchair users on the ground floor

Pantheon is situated on a busy street leading towards the Nieuwmarkt. Although there are not that many English language books held in stock here, this is a useful shop for local guides to Amsterdam and for picking up a British, French or American newspaper. They also have a good Dutch children's section and you can always order English books at the main desk.

101 Hieronymus Bosch

Leliegracht 36 ☎ (020) 623 7178
Open Thursday–Tuesday 11.30am–5.30pm
Tram 13, 14, 17 to Westermarkt and Leliegracht is around 5 minutes' walk away
It is difficult for wheelchair users to navigate round this small shop

This tiny but well stocked bookshop specialises in Medieval and Renaissance art and culture. Shelves are piled high with books on icons and Byzantine art and there is even a small section on the Vikings. This is a treasure trove for second-hand books as well as illustrated guides to the ancient world.

(102) Stadsboekwinkel

Vijzelstraat 32 ☎ (020) 625 0950 www.stadsboekwinkel.nl **Open** Tuesday–Friday 10am–5pm, Saturday, Sunday 11am–5pm **Tram** 16, 24, 25 to Keizersgracht
The bookshop is accessible via a lift into the building and adapted toilets can be found nearby

Located inside the monumental art deco building De Bazel (Amsterdam City Archives), this light and airy shop specialises in books, maps and objets d'art about Amsterdam. From limited edition black and white prints by local photographers to folding paper tulip vases, this is the best place to find both illustrated texts and imaginatively designed presents inspired by this beautiful city.

(103) Perdu

Kloveniersburgwal 86 ☎ (020) 422 0542 or 627 6295 www.perdu.nl **Open** Monday–Friday 1pm–6pm, Saturday 1pm–5pm **Metro** 51, 53, 54 to Nieuwmarkt **Tram** 4, 9, 14, 16, 24, 25 to Muntplein, both a 5-minute walk away
The shop is wheelchair accessible but the toilets at the rear have very narrow doors

Perdu is the only bookshop in Amsterdam specialising in poetry and it acts as a cultural magnet for writers. They stock poems by Dutch, English, German, Russian, Polish, Iranian and Spanish writers, amongst others. They hold occasional poetry readings and other literary events so Perdu is much more than just a place to buy books.

104 Architectura Natura

Leliegracht 22 ☎ (020) 623 6186
www.architectura.nl
Open Monday 12pm–6pm, Tuesday, Saturday 9am–6pm, Wednesday–Friday 9am–6.30pm
Tram 13, 14, 17 to Westermarkt, and Leliegracht is a 5-minute walk away
The ground floor is accessible but not the mezzanine above

A bibliophile's cornucopia, and an excellent place to browse for books on landscape and urban architecture. It is hard to leave the shop without finding something fascinating to read, and like in many specialist shops in the city, the staff is knowledgeable and interested in their subject.

Places to sit

🄝 Zorgvlied

Amsteldijk 273 ☎ (020) 540 4927
Free www.begraafplaatszorgvlied.nl or www.zorgvliedonline.nl
Open Monday–Friday 8am–4.45pm, Saturday, Sunday and bank holidays 10am–5pm
Tram 4 to Europaplein, 25 to President Kennedylaan
Metro to RAI
The cemetery is accessible but make sure you leave before the main gate shuts as the turnstile exit is not wide enough for wheelchairs

Built in the 19th century for the Borough of Amstelveen, this large open cemetery has many traditional memorials as well as few unusual modern headstones. The much-revered children's writer Annie G. Schmidt is buried here, as well as the notorious artist and singer Herman Brood. Located next to the River Amstel, this is a fascinating and yet relaxing place to go for a walk.

A literary route map (in Dutch) can be picked up from the Zorgvleid office.

106 Sporenburg Sculptures

P.E. Tegelbergplein **Free Open** all hours
Tram 10 to C. van Eesterenlaan, turn right into
Panamakade and walk alongside the water to the far end
of the island overlooking the mouth of the Amsterdam-
Rijnkanaal **Bus** 43 to RJH then walk over the Pythonbrug
The quay is wheelchair accessible but the cobbles make
the terrain uneven

These figurative sculptures were a delightful surprise when
discovered in the Zeeburg area, watching over the water on
the edge of a normally deserted quay. Apparently, the figures
are meant to be reminiscent of ancient Greek Kouri and
were made by the inventive Dutch artist Mark Manders.

107 Zoutkeetsplein

Zoutkeetsplein is on the corner of Barenzstraat and
Zoutkeetsgracht **Free Open** all day every day
Tram 3 to Zoutkeetsgracht **Bus** 48 to Barentszplein, then
walk down Barendszstraat to reach Zoutkeetsplein
The square is wheelchair accessible.

These beautiful animal sculptures can be found leaning on
the edge of a steel table just few minutes' walk outside the
central canals. A green copper ape with a long, curled tail
sits next to two languid gorillas – inspired street furniture
made by artist Merijn Bolink in 2005. On the quay nearby
are a few wooden benches overlooking the Westerkanaal,
making this a good place to watch passing boats.

108 Zoo-tje

The Zoo-tje is on the corner of Plantage Kerklaan and Plantage Doklaan **Free**
Open all day every day
Tram 9, 14 to Artis, then walk down Plantage Parklaan and the zoo-tje sculptures and small garden are on the right, just before the canal
The wooden benches at either end are wheelchair accessible

During the past few years this small patch of unkempt grass next to the Nijlpaardenbrug (Hippopotamus Bridge) has been transformed into a 'zoo-tje' (a mini zoo) by Burkina Fasoian artist Papa Adama. His recycled steel monkey, Tyrannosaurus Rex and kangaroo are a minor local attraction. This intriguing sculpture garden is only a minutes' walk away from the very crowded Artis Zoo yet feels very tranquil.

109 Expat Medical Centre

112 Bloemgracht ☎ (020) 427 5011
€ www.expatmc.net
Open Monday–Friday 9am–6pm
Tram 10 to Bloemgracht or 13, 14, 17 to Westerstraat then a 10-minute walk
The practice is wheelchair accessible, excluding the small toilet

This welcoming general practitioner's surgery is located on one of the prettiest canals in the Jordaan. Dr Cambridge doesn't only offer a range of services for tourists, however; long term or temporary residents can also make GP appointments or see the physiotherapist. The waiting room is not only free from muzac, it also doubles up as an art gallery and shows work by local printmakers and painters. Remember to bring your EHIC (European Health Insurance Card), or other insurance documents to obtain free treatment.

110 Nieuwe Ooster Begraafplaats and Museum Het Zover

Kruislaan 126 ☎ (020) 608 0608 **Free** www.totzover.nl
and www.denieuweooster.nl **Open** Monday–Friday
8am–5pm, Saturday, Sunday 10am–5pm. The museum is
open Tuesday–Sunday 11am–5pm except for major bank
holidays **Tram** 9 or **Bus** 40, 41, 136, 240 to Kruislaan
The cemetery and museum are wheelchair accessible

Built in 1894, this large graveyard is also a site of special
collections for both broadleaved and evergreen trees.
Near the entrance there is the unusual funeral museum,
Het Zover, which is a sensitively designed introduction to
how different cultures commemorate their dead.

111 Karthuizershof

Kaarthuizerstraat **Free**
Open all day every day
Tram 3, 10 to Marnixplein
The courtyard is wheelchair accessible

There are many delightful 'hofjes' or small courtyards
in Amsterdam and this is one of the least visited, so is
exceptionally quiet. Located near to the Noorderkerk, it
was built by the city architect Daniël Stalpaerts around
1650 as an almshouse for widows and unmarried
mothers. Leafy trees surround wooden benches, making
this a nice place to sit and read a book on sunny days.

⑫ Huis te Vraag

Rijnburgerstraat 51 ☎ (020) 614 3493
Free www.huistevraag.nl
Open Monday–Saturday 11am–5pm, Sunday 11am–2pm, closed during Christian but not secular bank holidays
Tram 2 to Zeilstraat **Bus** 23, 44, 145, 197 to Aalsmeerplein
The garden is wheelchair accessible but the ground can be uneven

Huis te Vraag is a delightful graveyard on the edge of the city full of rambling plants and ancient trees. It is no longer used for burials but is an entrancing place to wander. In one corner of this hidden garden there is a lovely view over open fields which makes the cemetery feel surprisingly rural. The use of mobile phones is not permitted in the grounds.

113 Westerstraat 327

De Jordaan **Free**
Open all hours **Tram** 3, 10 or **Bus** 18, 21 to Marnixplein
The courtyard is wheelchair accessible

This small 'hofje' (courtyard) is a surprising hidden oasis reached though a small alleyway on the western side of Westerstraat close to the Marnix sports complex. It is a good place to find a bench during the busy Monday morning street market on the main street. In summer the garden is full of spectacular pink hydrangeas and blackbirds searching for worms on the lawn. It is part of a private complex, however, so visitors need to be discreet and respect the privacy of the people who live here.

114 Hogeweg Fountain

Watergraafsmeer, at the corner of Linnaeusparkweg and Hogeweg **Free**
Open all day every day **Tram** 9 to Middenweg
The fountain is wheelchair accessible

In the middle of a quiet roundabout in a well-to-do neighbourhood in the east of the city there is a really nice place to sit and ponder. The Hogeweg Fountain is a simple Chinese yellow stone water feature, which in 2006 won 'The Golden Stone' for the best public space in Amsterdam. Surrounded by mature chestnut trees, it has been much appreciated by locals who come here to meet their neighbours or just watch the world go by.

Galleries

115 Paul Andriesse

Westerstraat 187 ☎ (020) 623 6237
Free www.paulandriesse.nl
Open during exhibitions Tuesday–Friday 11am–6pm, Saturday
2pm–6pm, and the first Sunday of the month 2pm–5pm
Tram 10 to Marnixplein
The gallery is wheelchair accessible

In 2011 Paul Andriesse Gallery moved to this grand building,
which is shared with renowned Dutch designer Marcel Wanders
upstairs. Work by internationally renowned artists is exhibited
here, from Rory Pilgrim's subtle, thoughtful installations to
the powerful yet tender figurative images by Marlene Dumas.
Natasja Kensmil's dark, historical drawings also make a visit to
this prestigious gallery a significant event. Don't forget to look
at the dramatic Bisazza tiled floor and the amazing geometric
light by Raymond Puts in the entrance to the building.

116 Galerie Bart

Bloemgracht 2 ☎ (020) 320 6208
Free www.galeriebart.nl
Open Wednesday–Friday 11am–6pm, Saturday and the first Sunday of the month 12pm–5pm, and by appointment
Tram 14, 17 or **Bus** 142, 170, 172 to Westerkerk
The gallery is wheelchair accessible

Since opening a few years ago, this gallery has proved to be a lively and imaginative newcomer to the Amsterdam art world. Their sister gallery in Nijmegen shows mainly work by artists at the start of their careers whilst the Amsterdam branch focuses on more experienced painters and sculptors. Using herself as a model, Tamara Muller paints compelling dystopian images of children and animals whilst Joyce van Dongen includes embroidery stitches in her extraordinary fictional landscapes. Galerie Bart also produce exquisite, beautifully printed catalogues which are worth a visit to the gallery in themselves.

117 Circle Gallery

Kerkstraat 67 ☎ (0) 654 378278
Free www.circlegallery.nl
Open by appointment
Tram 1, 2, 5 to Prinsengracht or Keizersgracht
The gallery and garden are wheelchair accessible

In 2009 the enterprising Melanie van Ogtrop converted a former coach house into a small non-profit gallery and beautiful sculpture garden. Both up-and-coming and established artists show work here, including Dr Judith Quax. Her photographs of the rooms lived in by Senegalese men who risk their lives travelling to Europe are poignant reminders of global inequality.

118 Galerie Clement

Prinsengracht 843–845 ☎ (020) 625 1656
Free www.galerie-clement.nl **Open** Wednesday–Saturday 11am–5.30pm **Tram** 16, 24, 25, to Prinsengracht
The ground floor of the gallery is accessible by wheelchair but not the first floor

This established gallery on the banks of the Prinsengracht canal specialises in contemporary prints. This is one of the few places in the west to see dramatic etchings by Chinese artist Ma Hui, who adds tangled red silk thread to her dense black ink etchings. Also try and catch a glimpse of Sandra Kruisbrink's delicate paper cuts of trees placed on painted landscapes.

119 Galerie Gist

Bloemgracht 82 ☎ (020) 622 6662
Free www.gistgalerie.nl
Open Wednesday–Saturday 1pm–6pm, and by appointment only during the summer
Tram 13, 14, 17 or **Bus** 142, 170, 172 to Westerkerk then walk up Prinsengracht, take the first bridge over the canal and turn left into Bloemgracht
The gallery is wheelchair accessible

Galerie Gist recently moved to the Jordaan after a few years on the banks of Het IJ. This unpretentious space shows work by up-and-coming as well as established Dutch artists. Gabriele Basch's complex abstracts such as her *Thinking of Sin* fill the canvas with a mixture of the decorative and carefully considered drips. Also look out for Seet van Hout's wonderful figurative artworks which combine blood-red watercolour stains with sewn portraits of female saints. A few non-Dutch painters also show here and this is a good space to see intelligent and sometimes challenging work by artists rarely seen outside the Netherlands.

120 Galerie de Witte Voet

Kerkstraat 135 ☎ (020) 625 8412
Free www.galeriedewittevoet.nl
Open Wednesday–Saturday 12pm–5pm, the first Sunday of the month 2pm–5pm
Tram 4, 16, 24 ,25 to Keizersgracht
The gallery is wheelchair accessible but the toilet is very small

The unredoubtable Annemie de Boissevain has been showing ceramic art for over thirty years in this former stable in the Kerkstraat, just round the corner from Amsterdam's antique quarter. The work shown in this tranquil space is consistently intriguing; keep an eye out for the sublime craftsmanship of Rem Posthuma and the wonderful sagging pink glazed ceramic girl's 'dresses' by Wilma Bosland. Exhibitions of contemporary art by mainly Dutch artists run throughout the year except during the summer months.

121 Fons Welters

Bloemstraat 140 ☎ (020) 423 3046
Free www.fonswelters.nl
Open Tuesday–Saturday 1pm–6pm
Tram 10, 13, 14, 17 to Rozengracht or
10 to Bloemgracht
The gallery is wheelchair accessible

Fons Welters Gallery is easily identified
from the exterior as it has large,
round, pale green fibreglass shapes
protruding from the front door. Behind
the entrance is a small project space
called 'Playstation' which often shows
installation pieces by younger artists.
At the rear there's a larger area covered
by a corrugated roof where intriguing
work such as Bjorn Dahlem's delicate
sculptures fill the unassuming space
(pictured). This is a good place to
see intelligent, engaging shows by
established or up-and-coming artists
of different nationalities. Look out for
former goldsmith Norbert Prangenberg's
exquisite vividly coloured paintings and
Maria Roosen's pendulous glass breasts.

122 De Appel

Eerste Jacob van Campenstraat 59
(entrance on the Ferdinand Bolstraat)
☎ (020) 625 5651
€ www.deappel.nl
Open Tuesday–Sunday 11am–6pm,
closed 30 April, 25 December and
during the installation of exhibitions
Tram 16, 24 to Stadhouderskade
There is no wheelchair access

Situated in the busy De Pijp area of
Amsterdam, this well-respected non-
commercial contemporary art space
tends to be overlooked by visitors,
perhaps because it mainly shows
conceptual or video work. The former
boys' school still retains a studious
atmosphere. Recent exhibitions have
included work by Valérie Mannearts,
whose curious wooden structures
and lumps on the gallery floor invite
us to discover the unexpected in
mundane things.

Places by water

(123) Nieuwe Meer

Nieuwe Meer can be reached by Nieuwemeerdijk, Oude Haagseweg or through Amsterdamse Bos
€ for ferry crossing **Open** all day every day
Bus 170, 172 to Koenenkade, walk past Spa Zuiver and Nieuwe Meer is to the right of the Bosbaan rowing lake
The paths are wheelchair accessible

The Nieuwe Meer (New Lake) has charming banks to walk along, many with sloping sandy beaches. This large stretch of water is surrounded by the Amsterdamse Bos with plenty of deciduous woodland on one side, and inland dunes on the other. A small boat ferries pedestrians and cyclists across the lake for €1 which is a nice trip, whether you need to get to the other side or not. The views from either bank are delightful, but if you can find someone to take you sailing, don't miss your chance to see the lake from the water.

124 Oeverlanden

Oeverlanden borders Nieuwe Meer
€ for ferry crossing
www.oeverlanden.nl
Open all day every day, ferry open 15 April–15 October, 12am–6pm Saturday, 11am–7pm Sunday and bank holidays
Tram 16, 24 to Ijsbaanpad, walk across the lock and cycle along the lake
Wheelchair users may need help getting on to the boat as there is a small step

'Oever' means riverbanks in Dutch, so this area bordering Nieuwe Meer is aptly titled 'Riverbanklands'. The sandy beaches are ideal for a simple picnic in summer whilst the grassland behind can feel quite wild and surprisingly untamed. Purple violets can be seen in spring along the Jaagpad, as well as other wild flowers such as silvery cinquefoil and common centaury. There is also a small ferry that carries foot and cycle passengers across the lake from April to October (follow the signs to the Veerpont). Anyone interested in natural history can join the organised walks to see dragonflies in the summer or beetles and fungi in the autumn.

125 De Poel

Entrances on Noordammerlaan and Handweg **Free**
Open all day every day
Bus 171 to Bovenkerk and get off near the church at the end of Noorddammerlaan, or 166 for the other entrance on the Laan Nieuwer Amstel near to the Raadhuis
The surrounding paths are wheelchair accessible

As the name suggests, De Poel is a very large pool located in the suburbs of Amstelveen. There are some lovely walks around the Grote (large) or Kleine (small) Poel, which are now part of a large nature reserve. This is an ideal place for bird watching, as there are grebes and other reed and water birds in abundance. In spring frogs can be heard croaking in the dykes and even semi-camouflaged brown hares can be spotted doing a bit of sunbathing in the long grass.

126 De Hoge Dijk

Abcouderstraatweg **Free**
Open all day every day
Metro 50, 54 to Holendrecht, walk or cycle past the AMC Hospital, parallel to the railway line, and the 'Recreatiegebied De Hoge Dijk' is on the left, about 10 minutes further on
The paths are wheelchair accessible

The English name for this tranquil nature reserve is 'High Dyke', and in this lush grassland you'll find numerous ponds and rivers, many renowned for their clear water. Amongst the tall reeds are some lovely flowers, such as the yellow dotted loosestrife and purple irises. It's difficult to believe that this undisturbed spot is only a few minutes' cycle away from one of the largest teaching hospitals in the Netherlands, but this is a very peaceful place to wander throughout the year.

⒓⒎ Nature Garden, Westerpark

Westerpark Natuurtuin, behind Westerpark, entrance on Haarlemmerweg 8–10
Free www.westergasfabriek.nl
Open all day every day
Tram 10, 22 or **Bus** 60 to Van Hallstraat
There are clearly defined paths but these may get muddy, making wheelchair access difficult

This nature garden has deep ponds and feels like a secret place despite being very close to the Westergasfabriek arts complex. In the very tall reeds and bushes you might see nesting wildfowl as well as toads and wild flowers. This hidden location feels like a wild haven in a city of many formal gardens.
Afterwards, you can sit outside in sunny weather and enjoy a drink at Pacific Park Cafe Restaurant (www.pacificparc.nl) in Polonceaukade 23, in the Westergasfabriek complex (it may be noisy inside, however).

128 Flevopark

Insulindeweg entrance near Javaplantsoen ☎ 0650 676339
Free www.flevopark.nl or www.nwediep.nl
Open Tuesday–Friday 3pm–8pm, Saturday, Sunday 12pm–8pm
Tram 7, 14 to Flevopark

Flevopark has a delightful atmosphere. With its green lawns, woodland paths and wild reed beds, this is a lovely place to go for an evening walk to watch the sun set over Nieuwe Diep Lake. Around eighty birds can be spotted here, from ungainly grey herons to bullfinches, lively house sparrows, willow warblers, ducks and swans. At the rear is the newly renovated Nieuwe Diep distillery which overlooks a large pond. This charming cafe serves home-distilled jenever, as well as beer, wine, apple cider, organic sheep cheeses, gourmet ox sausage and liverworst. Although it isn't in the centre, it really is worth discovering this beautiful green space on the edge of the city.

⑫⑨ Bosbaan

Bosbaanweg ☎ (020) 404 4869
Free www.debosbaan.nl
Open The paths around the Bosbaan are open all day every day
Bus 170, 171, 172 to Koenenkade **Metro** 51
Tram 5 to Van Boshuizenstraat, about 10 minutes' walk away, Bosbaan is the large stretch of water beyond the architecturally interesting (but rather expensive) wooden cafe
The cycle paths alongside the rowing lake are wheelchair accessible

This rectangular rowing lake is at its best in winter when people come to skate on the ice. If the water freezes very quickly, there may be solid rivulets on the surface, resulting in a quiet 'scritch scritch' sound as the skaters glide past with their arms neatly tucked behind them. At other times of the year, you can wander along the banks while admiring the national rowing team practicing their skills under the watchful gaze of grey herons.

130 Java Eiland

Walk between Javakade and Sumatrakade
Free www.amsterdamdocklands.com or
www.stadswandelkantoor.nl to arrange guided walks of
the area (**€** for guided tours) **Open** all day, every day
Tram 10 to Azartplain, walk eastwards at Bogortuin
The paths in-between the canals are wheelchair accessible

If you are interested in contemporary architecture, this
narrow island on Het IJ is one of the best places to
see impressive residential buildings. Starting from the
new media centre, De Pakhuis, walk or cycle over the
Kattenburgerstraat bridge and turn right when you reach
the cyclepath between Sumatrakade and Javakade Laan.

131 Silodam

Silodam, at the end of Westerdoksdijk
Free www.silodam.org to book a guided tour round the
building (**€** for guided tours) **Open** all day, every day
Bus 36 to Van Diemenstraat
The area around the Silodam is wheelchair accessible

Far away from any tourist routes, this windswept
peninsular is another place to discover some astonishing
contemporary architecture. Huge steel and glass
apartments dominate the skyline, some of which have
the IJ Meer swirling ominously underneath. Sitting on the
benches overlooking the water, this is the perfect place to
watch boats travel up and down with their various cargoes.

132 Henk John Botenverhuur

Dorpstraat 8, Holysloot ☎ (020) 490 4612

✆ www.john-botenverhuur.nl **Open** from mid-April–31 September Saturday, Sunday only 9.30am–6pm, in July and August open every day except Monday, Tuesday **Bus** 230 to Buikslotermeerplein then bus 30 to Holysloot, the last stop For wheelchair users it may be necessary to get assistance getting in and out of the boats. Small motor boats are also available for rent if rowing is difficult

Holysloot is a small Dutch village with a pretty white church about an hours' cycle from Amsterdam. At the end of the main street you'll find Henk John's boatyard on the edge of a lake to rent canoes, small rowing boats and motorboats. If you prefer to cycle, a tiny ferry (ring the bell to request a crossing) takes you over the lake to the Broek in Waterland cyclepath. On summer afternoons, you can row for hours without seeing another day-tripper. Just remember to duck very low in the boat when you go under the small cyclepath bridges. For somewhere to eat and drink, the former schoolhouse in the village has been converted into an attractive cafe and there are nice views of the dykes from the front or rear terraces. The only sounds you will hear outdoors are garrulous frogs croaking in the ditch.

133 The River Amstel

Amsteldijk **Free**
Open all day, every day
Tram 25 to Rijnstraat, walk to the end of the street and at the other side of Martin Luther Kingpark there is a rarely used road which runs along the banks of the river
Metro Wibautstraat, then turn into Grensstraat and at the end turn left into Wesperzide for a more urban walk
The footpaths are mainly wheelchair accessible, even in inclement weather

There are some very restful walks along the Amstel where the silence is only disturbed by the sound of coots and the flapping of swans' wings. The views are especially nice in the early morning or during winter when the reeds are still visible on the banks of the river. This is a lovely place to take a dog for a walk and watch the seasons change – especially when the fog gradually lifts in early spring.

34 Diemer Vijfhoek

Wim Noordhoekkade **Free**
Open all day, every day **Tram** 26 to Ijburg and Diemer Vijfhoek is around 30 minutes' walk away – take the small path down from Wim Noordhoekkade going towards Muiden, or cycle from Ijburg east towards Muiden along the Diemerzeedijk or through Diemerpark
The paths are unsuitable for wheelchairs

This may be one of the least visited places in Amsterdam but despite the urban growth of Ijburg nearby, it still feels quite wild and untamed. Unlike most parks or gardens in the Netherlands this remote peninsular seems rather neglected and shabby, but this adds to its charm.

135 Ponds near De Koenenkade

Koenenkade, between Nieuwe Meer and Amstelveenseweg
Free Open all hours **Bus** 142, 144, 170, 172 to Koenenkade, follow the path on the right towards the Nieuwe Meer
The paths are wheelchair accessible

Despite the presence of the tennis courts nearby, nature lovers still have some tranquil views of the small lakes in the woodland area en-route to the Nieuwe Meer. In winter, the fog gives a ghostly pallor to the trees and bushes which makes solitary walks seem quite romantic. Wildfowl gather here to replenish themselves on long journeys so greylag geese, the ubiquitous coot and an occasional swan can often be seen gliding on the water.

136 Buikslotermeer and Buiksloterkerk

Buiksloterkerkpad 10
Free www.buiksloterkerk.nl
Open all hours
Bus 34 to Barkpad or 37 to Fluitschipstraat, the church is a 6-minute walk away
The church is wheelchair accessible

Buikslotermeer is a lovely surprise for anyone who manages to cycle to the end of the Nooderpark. Surrounding the lake are pretty brick houses with wooden curved gables. Walking past these typically Dutch dwellings feels like wandering through a model village made up of neat dollhouses. There wasn't a lake here until the 1620s, made after the surrounding land was drained and turned into polders, and many of these houses were built around this time. The nearby Buiksloterkerk is also worth seeing. This small Protestant church with very high windows was renovated in 1710 and is now mainly used for temporary exhibitions and concerts.

⁽³⁷⁾ NDSM Pier

NDSM Pier **Free** www.ndsmhaven.nl **Open** all hours
Ferry 53 to NDSM Werf, when disembarking turn left on
Mt. Ondinaweg **Bus** 91, 94 to Klaprozenweg
The ferry is wheelchair and bicycle accessible

If you have had enough of pretty gardens and flower shops,
coming here is a good way to discover a more industrial
side to quiet Amsterdam. Take a free ferry ride to this
former ship building area then walk along a windswept
pier for interesting views of the city across the water.
Wander past the former Greenpeace boat and a pale grey
minesweeper to discover the red lighthouse ship opposite
Pollux, a 160-year-old sailing boat.

⁽¹³⁸⁾ Ijburg

Bert Haanstrakade **Free** www.ijburg.nl **Open** all hours
Tram 26 to Haveneiland West, turn left at Diemerparklaan
where you can follow the shore in either direction
There is good access for wheelchairs along the paths by
the shoreline

It might sound strange to be suggesting a brand new
housing development as a quiet place to walk, but this
recently built district of Amsterdam is surrounded by
water to the north and a nature reserve to the west.
There are some outstanding views at sunset along the
banks of the IJ Meer and it can almost feel as if you are
on the edge of a large inland sea.

139 Schellingwouderbreek

Volendammerweg **Free**
Open all hours
Bus 30, 32 to Volendammerweg and the lake is clearly visible on the right
The paths are wheelchair accessible but may get muddy in winter

This small lake is not only surrounded by pleasant woodland walks, it also leads on to the Koedijk path and the surprisingly verdant Baanakkerspark. Amsterdam Noord has a reputation for being an uninspiring place, but it is actually full of relatively unknown green spaces with inviting, tree-lined paths. Geese and other wildfowl flock together on the edge of the lake making this a good place for urban birdwatching.

140 Grote Vijver

Amsterdamse Bos (Bosbaanweg 5 for the visitor centre) ☎ (020) 545 6100
Free www.amsterdamsebos.nl
Open all day, every day, visitor centre open daily 12pm–5pm
Metro to Boshuizenstraat **Bus** 170, 172 to Koenenkade then follow the signs to the ponds
The paths are wheelchair accessible

Even on hot sunny days when Amsterdammers come here for walks, you'll find plenty of quiet paths along the Grote Vijver, the larger of the two small lakes in the Bos. There is even a small hill to climb up if you want a view of trees and a distant sky scraper. You can also hire rowing boats in the summer – another peaceful way to relax, far away from the city crowds.

Small hotels and B&Bs

141 Sloterkade Bed & Breakfast

Sloterkade 65 ☎ (020) 679 2753
www.bedandbreakfastamsterdam.net
Tram 2 to Amstelveenseweg **Bus** 15 to Harlemmermeerstraat
The rooms are not wheelchair accessible

This grand house has numerous beautifully decorated rooms and suites. The front bedrooms have views over the Schinkel canal and the B&B is very close to Vondelpark, so ideal for an afternoon stroll into town. Paul and Karen, the owners, are welcoming and friendly, and it is worth travelling out of the centre for their thoughtful touches. You'll find blackcurrant gin on arrival and breakfast is included in the overnight stay. Shoes are not allowed indoors, which helps to make nocturnal wanderings virtually inaudible but otherwise, birdsong and a passing boat are all you'll hear when staying in this gorgeous house.

142 Dumas and Considine

Roeterstraat 18 ☎ (020) 624 0174
www.amsterdambedandbreakfast.com
Tram 9, 14 to Plantage Kerklaan
No access for wheelchair users

This elegant 19th-century house has a spacious two
room apartment on the first floor, with nice views
overlooking both the street and the garden. Located near
to Amsterdam University Business School, the zoo and
museums in the Plantagebuurt, this is a good location for
cultural activities. The welcoming owners provide fresh
bread and fruit for breakfast but are very discreet, so this
lovely apartment feels very private and self-contained.

143 Le Maroxidien Bed & Breakfast

PrinsHendrikkade 534 ☎ (020) 400 4006 or (0) 611 873700
www.lemaroxidien.com **Bus** 22, 42, 43 to Prins
Hendrikkade, or a 10-minute walk from Central Station
It is impossible to enter the boat unless you are quite
nimble and the accommodation isn't suitable for children
under 6 years old

Sleeping on this atmospheric old boat you are transported
to different corners of the world. The three rooms, 'India',
'Morocco' and 'Mexico', are all decorated in bright colours
and have beautiful hand-carved furniture. A delicious
organic breakfast of fresh fruit, cereals, cream cheese and
bread is served in the large kitchen.

144 Kamer 1 Boutique Bed & Breakfast

Singel 416 ☎ (0) 654 776151

www.kamer01.nl

Tram 1, 2 ,5 to Spui

There is no disabled access as this is an old Dutch house with narrow stairs

There are only two rooms for guests in this stylish old canal house, but both are superbly decorated by the owner, one of Holland's foremost interior designers. Although the canal street below can be quite lively during the day, after dusk the rooms are very peaceful. Choose from the attic blue room with its circular bed or the sumptuous red room with its ornate carved wooden furniture. Guests can help themselves at any time to tea, coffee, organic juice and wines from one of the most beautiful small kitchens in Europe.

145 Synopsis Hotel

Nieuwe Keizersgracht 22a ☎ (020) 626 0075
www.synopsishotel.com
Metro and **Tram** Waterlooplein
There is disabled access to the ground floor rooms

This three star boutique hotel is located very close to
the Hermitage Museum on a quiet canal near to the
Amstel. It has two spacious rooms on the ground floor
and another on the first floor, but for a really quiet stay,
the garden room has a patio which overlooks the
pretty garden.

146 Sunhead of 1617

Herengracht 152 ☎ (020) 626 1809
www.sunhead.com
Tram 13, 14, 17 to Westermarkt or Dam or 1, 2, 5 to Dam
The building is not wheelchair accessible and no children
under 10 are allowed

Built in 1617, this remarkable former gentleman's
residence is one of the oldest heritage monuments on the
Herengracht. The house has been converted into separate
apartments, each with a distinctive colour scheme and
rooms full of objets d'art collected from around the world.
The interior design is outstanding, and with the old beams
and vaulted ceilings, it's like staying in a living museum.

⑭⑦ Triple Five Guest House

Prinsengracht 555 ☎ (020) 428 3809
www.triplefive.nl
Tram 1, 2, 5, 7, 10, 17 to Spui or Elandsgracht
The guest house is not wheelchair accessible

These bed and breakfast apartments have very simple interior design, with marble floors and few furnishings. The minimal style contrasts well with the ornateness of the surrounding buildings, many of which have sculpted cornices on the gables. Each of the rooms overlooks the canal and the street is surprisingly quiet, even during the summer. This is probably one of the most central guesthouses in the city and ideal for shopping in the 'negenstraatjes', where small boutiques line the streets that cut across the larger canals. The friendly owners will welcome you to their pristine guesthouse and tell you where to find the best places to eat, drink and walk in the area.

Hotel Ambassade

Herengracht 349 ☎ (020) 555 0222
www.ambassade-hotel.nl
Tram 1, 2, 5 to Spui
The majority of the rooms in the hotel are wheelchair accessible

At one time it its history, ten 17th-century houses were combined to create one of the most desirable hotels in Amsterdam. This charming canalside residence is the place to stay for writers, artists and culturally aware visitors from around the world. Perhaps one attraction is its excellent small library of books donated from former guests, or it may be the impressive collection of artworks produced by the COBRA group. From Theo Wolvecamp's dense black gouache works on paper to Jacqueline de Jong's colourful oils, the corridors and small reading rooms are full of rarely seen early 20th-century art. Many people walk straight through the etched glass entrance, unaware that this is also a beautiful artwork by Martin van Vreeden.

149 Raamgracht Bed and Breakfast

Raamgracht 23 ☎ (020) 627 3684

www.amsterdamcanalapartments.com

Tram 9, 14 or **Metro** 51, 53, 54 to Dam Square or Waterlooplein, then an easy walk to Raamgracht

The apartments are not wheelchair accessible

This attractive bed and breakfast apartment is located in one of the oldest parts of Amsterdam on one of the city's prettiest canals. There are delightful views over the water and it's often possible to catch a glimpse of coots nesting under the bridge nearby. The 17th-century houses have real character in this street and it will feel as if you are living like a local in one of these simply furnished apartments.

(150) **Burmanstraat Bed & Breakfast**

Burmanstraat 11 ☎ (020) 676 9239
www.bbamsterdam.nl
Metro 50, 51, 54 to Wibautstraat
There is no wheelchair access

Built in 1883, this studio apartment is very close to the River Amstel so is perfect for moonlight walks along the water. Although it is a 20-minute bike ride from the centre, it is worth booking a few nights here. Sam and Sjaak, the friendly owners, can accommodate up to four people so this is a good place for families who want some privacy. The modern kitchen and white mosaic tiled bathroom are well equipped, making this self-contained loft an inexpensive location for visitors.